How to Stop Being a Narcissist

Real and Proven Strategies to Change
Narcissistic/Manipulative Behavior and Stop
Sabotaging Your Relationships

Erik Parks

Table of Contents

Introduction

If you're wondering whether or not you're a narcissist, you're probably not one.

Given that you purchased this book, you must be wondering why I'm saying this. After all, you do believe you're a narcissist and want to learn more about this personality disorder. I'll tell you one thing, though: narcissists with full-blown personality disorders often fail to recognize their narcissism, especially if they aren't getting any sort of professional help. They believe their self-absorption is justified. Furthermore, those who lack empathy don't even realize it, and they continuously maintain their superiority over others.

As a growing number of people are becoming cognizant of the fact that narcissism is really a disorder, many narcissists may not even be aware of what it is. Unless they're explicitly confronted about it, narcissists are unlikely to believe that it might apply to them. Even when told they're narcissists, their reaction is typically vehement denial. By labeling their victims "narcissists" and denying it to those around them, they attempt to project revenge.

You should be aware that there are several degrees of narcissistic personality disorder (NPD). Only when a person encounters severe difficulties in daily life or demonstrates symptoms that motivate them to seek professional help is this disorder formally diagnosed. Many narcissistic people never get diagnosed.

The term "narcissist" is used to describe a wide variety of people, from those who simply display a few narcissistic traits to those who would be diagnosed with NPD. Most of us probably have some narcissistic tendencies. In certain ways, narcissism is even considered good. As a result, even though some of your actions may be motivated by narcissistic traits, you don't necessarily need to be diagnosed with NPD.

It's important to keep in mind that online tests are inaccurate at identifying narcissism or other mental health disorders in individuals. These tests don't represent a person's official diagnosis, even if they can help in gaining a general idea of a person's mental health. Only a licensed mental health professional is qualified to provide an accurate diagnosis. Your therapist will administer several personality tests that would assist in better understanding your thoughts and feelings and ascertaining whether or not you have narcissistic traits.

The most common tests utilized by therapists are:

- Personality Diagnostic Questionnaire-4 (PDQ-4)

- International Personality Disorder Examination (IPDE)

- Millon Clinical Multiaxial Inventory-III (MCMI-III)

Recognizing one's narcissistic tendencies is a critical and constructive step toward self-improvement. Accepting that one's behaviors, beliefs, or feelings point to narcissistic traits might be difficult but is nonetheless essential. Understanding how to control and keep an eye on those behaviors is beneficial. Narcissists that are willing to improve themselves are extraordinarily strong and resilient. They may acknowledge and admit both their strengths and their weaknesses.

At the moment, I won't go into great detail regarding narcissism's various traits, such as how grandiose, self-centered, and lacking in empathy narcissists are, or the different types of narcissism because we'll examine these concepts and characteristics in the next chapters. Instead, I want to look at narcissism from a whole different perspective.

Our narcissistic culture, which prioritizes being number one above everything else, exacerbates the issue. The importance of "making it" has surpassed that of fostering commitment, loyalty, integrity, and friendly relationships, leading to a trend of interpersonal exploitation.

Today, one of the easiest and most compelling ways to offend someone is by calling them "narcissists." We refer to people who're-domineering, boastful, entitled, or excessively content with their own lives as narcissists. One can wonder, though, if the term accurately characterizes the brash and arrogant individuals it typically alludes to. Upon closer examination, the anxiety and peacock behavior doesn't seem to be caused by feeling completely in love with oneself. On the contrary, it's not common for narcissists to value themselves highly. Because they can't be content with who they are, they boast and flaunt. They act out of dread of becoming ordinary people and being forgotten. Narcissism is often associated with vanity, greed, and lying, although these traits aren't indicative of self-love. Instead, they show that the person is devoid of any.

I wrote this book because I identify with your emotions and want you to know you're not alone. This book will assist you in creating a plan of action to get yourself out of this abyss of anxiety, fear, and depression. It can be a lifeline for anyone who's having emotional difficulties. It provides thorough details and helpful tips on how to control your anger and other emotions. Additionally, it offers advice on maintaining control over your thoughts and feelings and insight into why you feel the way you do. You'll discover several methods for overcoming narcissism, anger, and other emotional issues, such as:

- Identifying manipulative behavior

- Taking responsibility for your feelings

- Developing healthier communication styles and boundaries

- Learning how to express yourself assertively and respectfully

- Understanding the difference between healthy anger and unhealthy anger

- Defusing angry situations before they escalate

- Finding healthy outlets for stress, such as exercising or writing

This book will also teach you about "good narcissism." This is when a person discovers how to love oneself, which is a prerequisite for loving others. The majority of the world's problems are caused by people who don't believe in their worth. Because they've been raised to hate themselves and feel ashamed of who they are, these people are now unable to stop clamoring for the attention they were previously denied. Contrarily, those who're truly comfortable with themselves don't need frequent affirmation and live content lives.

We should strive to create a world in which more people value themselves. This is what's referred to as a "healthy narcissism" world. When we look in the mirror and like what we see, we'll be humble and self-effacing, prepared to love, care about and pay attention to others. We'll be kind and act selflessly toward those around us.

To improve their careers and interpersonal relationships, narcissists have to transform their behaviors. If they're happier and more successful, their friends and family, especially their kids, will greatly benefit. Narcissists can improve their lives by developing their humility, empathy, and patience. They should also learn to listen to other opinions without quickly rejecting them or seeking to justify their own. Additionally, admitting one's shortcomings can assist narcissistic people in developing a more self-aware and modest outlook on life. Finally, narcissists can build lasting relationships by having meaningful talks with other people and reaching out for assistance when necessary. These actions can help narcissists live happier lives and achieve greater success both personally and professionally.

Narcissists should focus on boosting their self-esteem by considering their skills and strengths and through positive self-talk. They can unwind and reestablish their sense of self by setting aside time each day for activities that promote relaxation and stress alleviation, such as yoga or meditation. Knowing one's limitations can also help one be more realistic about what one is capable of.

Last but not least, narcissists need to learn effective coping mechanisms to assist them in dealing with stress and depressive or anxious feelings. Regular exercise, keeping a journal, and spending time with supportive individuals who can offer solace and empathy are a few examples of these coping mechanisms. These suggestions can help narcissists make significant adjustments in their lives that'll result in more self-esteem and healthier relationships.

But I want you to understand that the transformation won't take place immediately. It can't be completed in a few hours, days, or months. It'll need effort and consistency from you to complete the long journey. Even though it might seem challenging, if you have the right mindset and approach, you can achieve your goals. The process requires your motivation and your desire to do better every day, and this is where this book can be of assistance. It'll help you escape the confines of your ego and offer direction on the path to a new self.

This book provides helpful guidance on breaking free from the narcissistic cycle and self-destructive behavior. It begins by examining the triggers, such as poor self-esteem and a need for acceptance, that set off narcissistic behavior. It then discusses how to begin the transformation process, including how to accept and love yourself for who you are as well as how to acknowledge your imperfections. The book also offers advice on how to improve interpersonal relationships as well as tools and tactics that help avoid engaging in narcissistic behavior. Narcissists can finally liberate themselves from their restraints, restore their independence, and lead happier and healthier lives with the help of this book.

Reparenting yourself or changing your personality and the traits you've been living with for a long time may seem impossible, but they're not.

Chapter 1:
How Are Narcissists Made?

W hat is narcissistic personality disorder (NPD)? What causes narcissism and how does this pattern develop? Is narcissism treatable? These questions and many more haunt not only the narcissistic victim but also the person with NPD.

Let's start with "What does personality mean and how does it develop?"

Dr. John Kim, an assistant professor of psychology and applied therapies at Lesley University, says that a person's personality comprises their "consistent ways of thinking, feeling, and acting that make them who they are." He believes that to study personality, you have to ask, "Why are most people usually the way they are?" Because this question is so broad, there are many ways to understand how personalities emerge and why people change over time.

No one knows how personalities come to be, but there are many theories. Below are some of the main ones:

1. **Psychoanalytic Theory by Sigmund Freud:**

   This theory states that personality shows how the unconscious mind works. In his book *Introduction to Psychoanalysis*, written in 1920, Freud thought that a person's personality was made up of three parts, each serving a different purpose: id, ego, and super-ego.

   The id is responsible for people's basic instincts, natural urges, and personalities. It has nothing to do with the conscious mind.

- The ego also called the "self," uses judgment to help the id get what it wants. It works with the mind or without.

- The super-ego is in charge of morality and how pride and guilt are used. It's both in the conscious and unconscious mind.

2. Humanistic Theory by Abraham Maslow:

In the 1950s, Abraham Maslow came up with the humanistic theory. He thought that Freud's psychoanalytic theory was wrong because it focused on people with bizarre personalities. Maslow instead emphasized how important it was to understand the mind and personality in their normal states.

The humanistic theory says that people have free will and make decisions based on their desire to be the best they can be. People's personalities comprise their experiences and interactions with their surroundings.

Humanistic theories of personality ultimately led to Maslow's famous *Hierarchy of Needs*. Based on this theory, more complex needs arise as the basic ones are met.

According to Maslow, five needs exist and they're explained in his book *Motivation and Personality*, written in 1954. In order of most needed to least, those are:

1. Self-actualization: morality, creativity, spontaneity, acceptance, experience purpose, meaning, and inner potential

2. Self-esteem: confidence, achievement, respect for others, and the need to be a unique individual

3. Love and belonging: friendship, family, intimacy, and sense of connection

4. Safety and security: health, employment, property, family, and social stability

5. Physiological: breathing, food, water, shelter, clothing, and sleep

3. Trait Theory by Gordon Allport:

Allport's best-known book on trait theory was *Personality: A Psychological Interpretation*. It says that a person's personality comprises a collection of traits. These traits help show what makes each person unique and can be put into three main categories:

- Cardinal traits: They are highly prevalent, dominant traits that affect almost everything about a person's behavior and personality. These aren't common.

- Central traits: They are five to ten traits that describe the most important things about a person. Intelligence and shyness are two examples.

- Secondary traits: They depend on the situation. One example could be liking certain foods or colors more than others.

4. Social Cognitive Theory by Albert Bandura:

Bandura's theory says that people's personalities are shaped by their social situations. They're based on two key ideas:

- People's inner thoughts, surroundings, and actions all affect each other.

- People are best known for three types of cognitive capabilities: those that help them make mental pictures of events, think about themselves, and improve themselves.

The social cognitive theory also states that people learn about themselves by watching others act. This leads to adaptation and assimilation, especially if those behaviors are rewarded.

People often think of the social cognitive theory as a bridge between personality theories that focus on behavior and those that focus on how people think.

How do the four theories work in the real world?

- The psychoanalytic theory encourages clinicians to treat patients in a "past-focused" way and "below the surface." Counselors often look at their clients' early lives to help them better.

- The humanistic theory tells counselors to look at their clients' problems in the present.

- The scientific study of personality can learn much from the trait theory (as opposed to therapeutic services). It lets researchers see how traits, thoughts, feelings, and actions are related.

- Researchers can learn more about social psychology with the help of the social cognitive theory. It lets them study how different situations can make people act in ways that don't fit

  their personalities.

When a person's personality gets in the way of their daily life, this is called a disorder. The Mayo Clinic says that fixed or unhealthy ways of thinking, acting, or functioning mark a personality disorder.

Clinicians often use two main types of tests to figure out a person's personality: objective tests and projective tests.

There are three main categories of personality disorders:

1. Cluster A disorders where people behave and think strangely. There are three types of personality disorders in this category and they are: paranoid, schizotypal, and schizoid.

2. Cluster B disorders are characterized by actions and thoughts that are too emotional or unpredictable. NPD, antisocial personality disorder and borderline personality disorder are examples of disorders in this category.

3. Cluster C disorders are characterized by anxious, fearful thinking or behavior. Some examples in this category are avoidant personality disorder, dependent personality disorder, and obsessive-compulsive personality disorder.

Personality disorders change how a person thinks, acts, and talks to others. The American Psychiatric Association says that the main signs of personality disorders are impairments in "self" functioning, problems in relationships, and maladaptive patterns of thinking, feeling, and behaving.

The psychoanalytic theory, especially the object-relations and self-psychology models, gave rise to the first ideas about narcissism. The object-relations model says that people are driven by two main things: lust and anger. It also assumes that people have self-representations, mental pictures of themselves, object representations, or mental pictures of things. These representations can be good (caused by sexual drive) or bad (caused by fear or aggression). How people combine positive and negative self - and object - representations, leads to various manifestations of narcissism in their lives (Kernberg, 1975).

Healthy narcissism occurs when both positive and negative self - and object - representations exist. It lets people realistically judge themselves and others. On the other hand, pathological narcissism happens when people only see the good in themselves and project their negative self - and object - representations onto others. People with pathological narcissism have an overly positive or grandiose view of themselves and a very negative or contemptuous view of others.

Heinz Kohut, a psychoanalyst, and psychiatrist, came up with his self-psychology model in 1971. His model says that children are born with self-love, called "primary narcissism." Young children think very highly of both themselves (the "grandiose self") and their parents (the idealized parent image). Later, the grandiose self becomes more mature and lays the groundwork for growing self-esteem and ambition. The idealized image of a parent becomes the "super-ego," a set of moral standards and values that affect the values a person grows to hold. When children's needs aren't met well enough by their parents, for example, the grandiose self and the idealized parent image may remain in their infantile forms and lead to pathological narcissism. As a result, the self-psychology model regards narcissism as a type of stalled development. Narcissists may try to make up for their unmet social needs later in life by trying to get too much attention from their family, friends, or romantic partners.

As time passes, narcissists use various methods to cope with their inner struggles. They shape their relationships with other people by trying to get their attention and admiration. For example, they move quickly to be the center of attention or show that they're better than others. On an individual level, narcissists try to confirm their high opinions of themselves by taking too much credit for their successes, ignoring their bad traits, overestimating their skills and accomplishments, and rewriting their pasts in ways that make them look good.

Ironically, though, narcissists may end up hurting themselves by trying to be too big. Their hard work and dedication to getting attention and admiration often turn off the people they want to like them. When other people notice a narcissist's self-centeredness, manipulativeness, arrogance, or bad temper, they stop being the source of validation that narcissists need. This has been called the "ultimate narcissistic paradox" because narcissists can't help but be self-centered, manipulative, arrogant, or angry (Morf & Rhodewalt, 2001).

Narcissism is a long-term pattern of urges and behaviors that are very similar to the urges and behaviors of addiction. In particular, narcissism can be like an addiction in that it can cause cravings, withdrawal, and tolerance.

- Cravings are strong desires for something or someone that you want. Narcissists want to be liked by everyone and will do anything to get what they want.

- Withdrawal is the feeling of discomfort that happens when you stop getting something you want, like a drug. When narcissists don't get the attention they want, they often get angry and aggressive, just like addicts do when they can't get their fix.

- Tolerance is when the effects of a stimulus get weaker over

  time, so you have to take more of it to get the same results. Narcissists often seem unable to get enough attention and usually want more praise from more people.

An inflated sense of self-importance, a need for appreciation and attention, and a lack of empathy for others are what characterize a narcissist. Some research suggests that certain personality traits, such as a need for power and control, may be more common in people with NPD. It's also thought that people who've experienced emotional abuse or neglect or have been excessively praised or idolized may be more likely to develop narcissistic traits. However, it's essential to note that not all people who've experienced those will go on to become narcissists.

There's no one-size-fits-all explanation for what makes a narcissist. It's a complex and multifaceted disorder that's influenced by a range of factors. Recent studies have shown that four factors can lead to

NPD.

1. Hereditary Factor

Studies show that some people are more likely to have NPD because of their genes. They might not develop narcissistic traits, but if they're exposed to certain risk factors, they might be more likely to do so.

Personality traits like grandiosity and a sense of entitlement, often found in people with NPD, can be inherited. The type of NPD a person has may also be affected by their genes. Parents with NPD won't necessarily pass on these traits to their kids, but the fact that they have them could make it more likely for their kids to have them.

2. Parenting Factor

Some studies have found that NPD is linked to many parenting styles. Some bad parenting habits, like neglect, mistreatment, and abuse, are done on purpose, but other bad habits can come from parents who wish well for their children.

Further research has shown that grandiose and vulnerable narcissism is more likely to happen when people are overprotected. There's also a link between NPD and parents overvaluing or being too easy on their children. Children who get too much praise for their accomplishments or who don't have limits are more likely to show traits linked to NPD as they age.

Most of the time, narcissism and personality traits are caused by problems with development. These are things that happen to kids and adults alike. It mostly shows what happened to the person when they were young and in their teens. We start to become who we are as soon as we're born. Up until our mid-20s, our brains change quickly. This is when we go through childhood and adolescence. In our mid-20s, things slow down a bit. By the time we're in our mid-20s, our personalities are pretty solid.

People with narcissistic personalities frequently have negative experiences and suffer post-traumatic stress disorder. Children's personalities are shaped by neglect, abuse, and inconsistency, and some patterns of narcissism are similar to those of post-traumatic stress disorder. It's common for people who've been through trauma to have trouble expressing their feelings, have a constant fear of danger, or act on impulse.

Attachment problems can also be a sign of narcissism. Early on, children require dependable adults to assist them in learning important skills and feeling secure in themselves and their surroundings. Attachment styles like self-regulation, which are linked to anxiety and avoidance, are also linked to narcissistic behavior. So, the person never felt safe in close relationships, not as a child nor as an adult. There's always this push and pull between them coming in and going out, and it's hard for them to get close and stay close.

Despite the many effects parenting has on kids, it's critical to remember that no one method of raising a child can cause NPD. Even though some ways of parenting are associated with higher levels of narcissism, parenting isn't always the cause of NPD. The same factors that contribute to narcissism can also contribute to other disorders. Moreover, it often happens that in the same family, not all siblings develop NPD even though they've lived in the same house and were raised by the same parents.

3. Environmental Factor

The environment a person grows up in, including their culture and way of life, could also cause NPD. Mistreatment as a child seems to increase the chance of NPD in early adulthood. Studies also show that people with narcissistic traits might be more common in cultures that value individuality.

Parenting is a big part of a child's environment, but other factors can also affect how likely they are to develop NPD as an adult. For example, some people bullied as kids may be more likely to develop narcissistic traits, especially if the bullying continues for a long time.

Researchers have found that criticism from teachers and other authority figures, can have the same effect as criticism from parents. Because people with NPD are more likely to need more from their caregivers, they tend to grow up in environments where they're constantly praised for everything (without rules, boundaries, or structure) or where they're traumatized or abused at a young age and don't have the skills to deal with their environment's flaws.

4. Biological Factor

According to recent research, biological factors may also play a role in the occurrence of NPD.

People with NPD have high levels of oxidative stress, an imbalance of molecules that can stress the body. Brain scans show that people with NPD have less gray matter in the parts of the brain that are responsible for empathy. Neuroscientists have also found a connection between NPD and differences in the structure of the prefrontal brain. More research needs to be done, but in the future, it might be possible to look at someone's brain and tell if they have narcissistic personality traits.

Some researchers think NPD could be caused by how someone looks or how they're built. Higher levels of narcissism are linked to being good at sports, looking good, and being strong. After all, appearance is one thing people think shapes who they are. Other elements could make the risk of NPD higher. For example, NPD is diagnosed in men more than in women, which suggests that men may be more likely to have this mental health condition.

In summary, we know for sure that researchers have found links between NPD and some parenting styles, experiences, and cultures, but these factors aren't the same for everyone with NPD. There could be a combination of those factors for each case. For example, someone with narcissistic traits may be more likely to get NPD if exposed to other risk factors because of their genes or biology.

Even though experts have found these risk factors, we still don't know what causes NPD. You can avoid some factors, but there's no surefire way to stop the disorder. One thing we know for sure is that narcissism leads to a deep sense of shame and pain. People with NPD are very sensitive to criticism or loss because they have low self-esteem. Criticism can make people feel humiliated, degraded, hollow, and empty, even if they don't show it. They might respond with contempt, anger, or a defiant attack known as a narcissistic injury. In the next chapter, you'll know more about narcissistic injuries.

Chapter 2:
What Is a Narcissistic Injury?

W hat is an injury in general? It's anything that hurts and harms us. We typically reserve this term for something more physical, like a bruise, a burn, or a broken bone. So that then begs the question, can injuries be psychological? Yes, they can. Someone can hurt your feelings or an incident can hurt your pride. Just like a physical injury, a psychological injury also results in pain. It's a psychological pain, but it's a pain nonetheless.

Intriguingly, neuroimaging studies reveal that psychological pain in our brains resembles physical pain. What happens when your ego is injured? That may occur when someone criticizes you, comments about something important to your identity, or exploits a weakness of yours. At some point, we all get our egos injured, but narcissists overreact to the same situation and their injury will be full-blown. That is what a narcissistic injury is.

A narcissistic injury is typically an overreaction to perceived or minor criticisms that injure a narcissist's fragile ego. It's a perceived threat to a person's self-esteem or self-worth. It can occur when someone's sense of self-importance is challenged, or their delusions of grandeur are deflated. This can cause the person to feel humiliated, rejected, or injured and may trigger various negative emotions, including anger, aggression, and depression. The concept of a narcissistic injury is often used in the context of NPD.

No matter how small something may seem to emotionally stable people, it's not to narcissists. To an insecure person, it can threaten their entire sense of self-worth. Now, the healthiest people out there might get a little bit defensive in these situations and then see that it's not that big a deal. They let it go and move on. A narcissist, on the other hand, will probably never forget that little incident. But what makes an ego injury turn into a full-blown narcissistic injury? Those two terms, ego injury, and narcissistic injury can be somewhat synonymous for a narcissist.

Let's suppose Johan has worked for a trucking company for four years. His self-centered nature makes him difficult to deal with. He started as a driver, moved to a lower-level management position, then to a middle-level management position, and is now being considered for an administrative role in upper management. This is the position he believes he deserves. Undoubtedly, he can do a better job than the current management because he has worked harder than anyone else. In the end, a colleague with a quick mind gets the job instead of him, so he has to remain in middle management. He gets a narcissistic injury when he thinks he is less qualified than his colleague. This goes against his high opinion of himself and hurts his ego.

Another example is Sara, a narcissistic mother, who was a talented basketball player when she was younger. She wanted to play in the WNBA, but people told her she wasn't good enough. She wishes she could travel back in time and show her coaches, scouts, and teammates how wrong they were about her and that they didn't see how capable she was. She can't turn back time to live out this dream, but now that her daughter plays basketball, she can live it through her. Sara makes it to all her daughter's practices and games and trains her. From the outside, Sara seems like a great mom helping her daughter follow her dreams. But Sara isn't doing it for her daughter. She's doing it for herself. She wants to feel great, and she wants to show everyone that they've been wrong about how talented she is. She is a self-centered mother living her dream through her daughter. Sara's daughter tells her one day that she has lost interest in basketball and won't be playing in college. Instead of supporting her daughter, Sara experiences a narcissistic injury. This is because she has been living through her daughter for so long to fulfill her dream that her daughter's decision feels like an attack on her false identity.

There are many potential examples of narcissistic injuries, as the concept can apply to various situations and individuals. Here are a few examples:

- A child constantly criticized or belittled by a parent may develop feelings of worthlessness and inadequacy, leading to a narcissistic injury.

- An employee who's passed over for a promotion, despite feeling confident in their abilities and expecting to be recognized for their hard work, will experience a narcissistic injury.

- A romantic partner who's constantly criticized or belittled by their spouse may begin to feel that they're not good enough, leading to a narcissistic injury.

- A person admired and idolized by others may experience a narcissistic injury if faced with criticism or rejection, as it challenges their sense of self-importance.

Potential triggers for a narcissistic injury depend on the individuals and the incidents they encounter. In general, a narcissistic injury is triggered when a person's sense of self-importance or self-esteem is threatened or challenged in some way. The threats could be real or perceived. The most common triggers are:

- Criticism or rejection: People may experience a narcissistic injury if they feel criticized or rejected by someone they admire or respect. This can be particularly damaging if the person has fragile self-esteem.

- Failure or disappointment: A person may experience a narcissistic injury if they feel they've failed at something important or are disappointed by their performance. This can be especially difficult if the person has high expectations for themselves.

- Envy or jealousy: A person may experience a narcissistic injury if they feel that someone else is more successful or accomplished than they are. This can be especially difficult for people with a strong need for admiration or attention from others.

- Loss of control: People may experience a narcissistic injury if they feel they're losing control over an important aspect of their life, such as a job, a relationship, or a personal project. This can be especially difficult for people with a strong need for control.

People who experience a narcissistic injury may feel a range of negative emotions, including:

- Humiliation: A person may feel humiliated or embarrassed if their self-importance is challenged or deflated.

- Rejection: A person may feel rejected or abandoned if they feel that someone they admire or respect is critical of them or doesn't value them.

- Worthlessness: A person may feel that they're not good enough or have failed somehow, which can lead to feelings of insignificance and inadequacy.

- Anger: A person may feel angry or frustrated if they feel their sense of self-worth has been threatened or challenged.

- Aggression: A person may become aggressive or lash out at others if they feel that their self-esteem has been damaged.

- Depression: A person may feel depressed if they don't meet their expectations or struggle to cope with feelings of worthlessness or rejection.

Everyone reacts differently to a narcissistic injury and the specific feelings that a person experiences may vary depending on their circumstances and personality.

The duration of a narcissistic injury can vary widely, depending on various factors, including the individual's personality, coping skills, and the specific circumstances that triggered the injury. If a person has a strong sense of self-worth and healthy coping skills, they may be able to process their feelings and move on from a narcissistic injury more quickly. Then again, if a person has a fragile sense of self-esteem and lacks effective coping strategies, they may struggle to recover from a narcissistic injury and continue to feel hurt and wounded for longer.

In addition to criticism, disagreement, and a challenge to the narcissist's perceived superiority, various events can trigger narcissistic injury. In most cases the narcissistic injury is followed but what is known as narcissistic rage. When a narcissist experiences narcissistic rage, they may become hostile or violent and try to manipulate or control the person they perceive to be a threat.

There are two kinds of narcissistic rage: explosive or outward rage and passive or inward rage. A narcissist can experience both types.

- Explosive rage: The person throws insults, screams, and yells and may even threaten others or hurt themselves.

- Passive rage: The person sulks and refuses to talk to others.

According to psychiatrist Adam Blatner, anger goes through seven stages:

1. Stress: Feelings of anger that are just below the surface and aren't acknowledged or dealt with.

2. Anxiety: Small signs of anger start to show up.

3. Agitation: Signs of unhappiness start to emerge without being able to say why.

4. Irritation: Showing more displeasure to get others to react and change.

5. Frustration: Having a mad face or saying mean things to show anger.

6. Anger: Speaking louder and showing more emotion.

7. Rage: When someone loses their temper and gets extremely angry.

Narcissistic anger or rage, on the other hand, doesn't build up over time; it's instant. The person goes straight from feeling stressed to expressing full-blown anger, either outward or inward.

Narcissistic rage can appear in several ways, and the manifestation depends on the individual and the situation. Some common ways that narcissistic rage can manifest include:

- Anger: The person may become visibly angry and lash out at others with verbal or physical aggression.

- Control: The person may try to control or manipulate the situation or the people around them to protect their ego.

- Denial: The person may deny that anything is wrong or that they're experiencing any negative emotions.

- Blaming others: The person may blame others for their problems or negative emotions rather than take responsibility for their actions.

- Projection: The person may project their negative qualities onto others rather than acknowledge their flaws.

- Passive-aggression: The person may express their anger indirectly through passive-aggressive behaviors, such as sulking or withholding affection.

- Gaslighting: The person may try to manipulate others by denying reality or manipulating the truth to protect their ego.

Narcissists pay a high price for their rage and behavior. This can come in the form of one or more of the following:

- Family distancing: Many studies have examined the link between narcissism and troubled relationships with family.

- Breakup of relationships and divorce: Research has also shown that narcissism negatively affects romantic relationships and marriages.

- Cutting off relationships: Since narcissists prefer to "use" people instead of "relate" to them, they tend to leave behind a lot of broken relationships. Narcissists also lose relationships because people feel let down, disappointed, lied to, used, manipulated, violated, exploited, betrayed, ripped off, put down, invalidated, or ignored.

- Loneliness and isolation: Because of the above three, most narcissists have few, if any, healthy, close, and long-lasting relationships. Some high-functioning narcissists do well in life, but it's at the expense of others, and when they get to the top, they're all alone.

- Lost chances of friendship: Because of a lack of real essence or sense of connection in a relationship.

- Trouble with money, career, or the law: Because narcissists broke the rules, were very careless, indulged themselves without thinking, or did other mistakes.

- Damaged reputation: This can be caused by a lack of credibility, reliability, and trustworthiness in their personal or professional life.

- A deep-seated fear: Of being rejected or of not being important.

Now that you know what narcissistic rage is all about, it's necessary to mention that narcissists worry that people might not see them as the privileged, powerful, popular, or "special" people they want to be. When their fears are confirmed, they react very strongly. Even if they don't want to acknowledge it, many narcissists feel like the "ugly duckling" deep down.

Now that you understand that a narcissistic injury is a disproportionate reaction to an often very benign comment or situation, you might be wondering, do narcissists ever hit rock bottom?

"Rock bottom" is often used when talking about addictions. When a person who's addicted to drugs hits a point where they realize they have to change or they might end up dying, this is called a "time of recognition." Many addicts realize that they have to do something, that this is it, and that they can't just keep looking for one more hit. They don't reach that decision just because their friends, doctors, or therapists told them to, or their families intervened. They want to do that change. It takes time and commitment to recover and stay clean for a long time. And for some people, hitting rock bottom isn't always the end, but it's often the best place to start. Anyone who wants to stay sober for a long time and is willing to work hard every day can do so. That often means a big change in how people live. It could mean a new job, a new line of work, a new place to live, some new friends, or a new life free from addiction.

Not every narcissist will hit rock bottom. Some do, but not all, just like some addicts die from an overdose or get sick before changing their lifestyle. Most narcissists, who go through these terrible losses or fall from fame or success, will spend the rest of their lives feeling angry, resentful, and like the world is out to get them. In these situations, their lowest point leads to a lonely, angry, and isolated life, with most of their bridges burned. But some narcissists fall, and then stop to think about themselves and their lives. They start to see how they contributed to the mess they've made. They become humble, take responsibility, and try to make things right. Making amends could mean reaching out to people and admitting their mistakes. But making amends may also mean stepping out of the spotlight, no longer needing to be the center of attention, giving up some of their superficial nonsense, closing their social media accounts, listening to other people when they talk, being more mindful, and taking pleasure in the little things they never noticed or were annoyed by before.

Change is possible, but it takes time and effort. You have to do it every day and believe in it. Narcissistic injuries can significantly impact a person's emotional well-being and lead to negative emotions and behaviors. If you're striving to cope with a narcissistic injury, it may be helpful to seek support from a mental health professional who can help you work through your feelings and develop healthy coping strategies.

You can try to protect yourself from narcissistic damage in different ways:

- Work on boosting your self-esteem: Having a powerful feeling of self-worth and self-esteem will make you feel more resilient and better able to cope with any criticism or rejection that may be sent in your direction. Try to be sympathetic and kind to yourself, and center your attention on your positive qualities and achievements.

- Establish appropriate limits: Establishing appropriate limits and boundaries with people and explaining your needs and expectations is essential. This can make you feel more in charge of your relationships and can lessen the likelihood that others will hurt or disappoint you. It can also help you feel more assertive in handling difficult situations.

- Develop healthy coping skills: Having healthy coping skills, such as mindfulness, relaxation techniques, and seeking support from others, can help you manage your emotions and bounce back more quickly if you experience a narcissistic injury. These skills can also help you avoid experiencing a narcissistic injury in the first place.

- Seek help: If you find it difficult to manage the effects of a narcissistic injury, it may be beneficial for you to seek support from a mental health professional, a trusted friend, or a family member. Talking about your feelings with someone you trust and seeking their views on the situation helps a lot.

- Isolate if it's essential: If you're feeling like a time bomb that's about to go off, it's best to spend some time alone so that the amount of collateral damage is minimized. When the phase in which you felt easily triggered or angry has passed, put your resilience to the test by getting back into your relationships.

It's important to note that it may not always be possible to completely avoid a narcissistic injury, as it can be triggered by a wide range of circumstances and may be beyond your control. However, taking steps to protect yourself and develop healthy coping skills can help you manage your emotions and recover quicker when you experience a narcissistic injury.

Also, as I've mentioned earlier, narcissistic injury and narcissistic rage are feelings that can arise in individuals with narcissistic traits. It's important to recognize and understand narcissistic traits. As you go on reading, you'll be able to fully understand NPD and learn about the various aspects of this disorder. In the next chapter, we will delve further into narcissism, its various characteristics, and its diagnosis.

Chapter 3:
Are You a Narcissist?

D o you recall the first sentence in the book? "If you're wondering whether or not you're a narcissist, you're probably not one." This chapter is going to help you find out if you're a narcissist or not.

In our selfie-obsessed, celebrity-driven culture, the word "narcissism" is often used to describe someone who seems too vain or full of themselves. But from a psychological point of view, narcissism isn't the same as self-love. People with NPD are more likely to be in love with a grandiose, idealized version of themselves. They love this inflated sense of themselves because it keeps them from feeling insecure. But it takes much work to keep up their delusions of grandeur, which is where their dysfunctional attitudes and behaviors come in.

People with NPD display a pattern of egocentric, arrogant thinking and behavior, a lack of empathy and care for others, and a strong need to be admired. People with narcissistic tendencies will always feel like they deserve something, whether it's a raise in pay, a promotion, or even the best seat on an airplane.

The most common trait of narcissists is the need for attention. When narcissists aren't the center of attention, they may get angry and start a fight. This feeling of being owed something could last for the rest of their lives.

Narcissists are very manipulative. They do whatever they can to force others to do what they want, no matter what. If people do something they don't like, they'll try to cut them off or call them rude.

Narcissists often talk in a way that shows how important they think they are and how much they want to be liked. Some phrases that narcissists tend to use are:

- "I'm the smartest, most successful, most attractive, or best person you know." Narcissists often try to make other people think they're better by bragging about what they've done or overstating their abilities.

- "You should feel lucky to have me in your life or be around me." Narcissists often expect special treatment and may make others feel as though they're lucky to be in the narcissist's presence.

- "I don't have time for this. I have more important things to do." Narcissists often prioritize their own needs and may dismiss the needs or concerns of others as unimportant.

- "I'm always right. I never do anything wrong." Narcissists often have a rigid and unchanging view of the world and may think they're never wrong.

- "I can't believe you didn't do or couldn't do X better." Narcissists may have high expectations of others and criticize or belittle others when they don't meet those expectations.

Emotionally stable people often say that people with NPD are arrogant, scheming, selfish, condescending, and demanding. This way of thinking and acting shows up in every part of a narcissist's life, including work, friendships, family, and romantic relationships.

People with NPD resist modifying their behavior, even when it's causing them problems. They tend to blame other people. Moreover, they're very sensitive, and even the smallest criticisms or disagreements, which they see as personal attacks, make them angry. People close to narcissists often find it easier to do what they want to avoid their anger and coldness. Knowing more about NPD is the key to identifying narcissists in your life, protecting yourself from their power games, and setting better boundaries.

How well or how poorly someone listens are good indications of whether they're narcissistic. Someone who tries to figure out what's interesting and makes sense in other people's words is likely to be emotionally healthy. Dismissing or ignoring what other people say is a sign of narcissism. Being all about other people can also be a problem. Too much kindness can lead to codependency. People who're healthy and have healthy relationships can listen to their concerns and those of others. They can be self-centered (taking care of themselves) and selfless (paying attention to what others want).

I call being able to hear yourself and other people "bilateral" listening. When disagreements arise, listening to both sides helps find solutions that work for both. This keeps the goodwill in their relationships going. For example, if you felt tired, you would pay attention to that and go to bed. Similarly, if a friend has a problem and needs to talk to you immediately, you might suggest the two of you talk for a few minutes before going to bed and then talk in the morning. That could work out well for everyone. If you lean toward narcissism, on the other hand, you might tell your friend right away, "No, I'm too tired." One-sided listening is what narcissistic listening is. All that matters is what the narcissist wants, thinks, or feels. What others want, think, or feel isn't important information.

If you suspect that you're a narcissist or have narcissistic tendencies, the quiz below will help you determine if you're one, and it does that based on some basic characteristics of narcissism discussed earlier. Give each question a score between 0 and 5. You can start by doing the quiz yourself. Then go back and score someone hard to deal with in your life. The goal is to see your own and other people's patterns. Clarity and honesty here are big steps toward being able to make positive changes.

Q1. Do you frequently discuss yourself and your accomplishments while not showing much interest in others?

Score: _____

0 - I rarely or never talk about myself and make an effort to show interest in others.

1 - I sometimes talk about myself and my accomplishments, but I also make an effort to show interest in others.

2 - I often talk about myself and my accomplishments, but I also make an effort to show interest in others.

3 - I mostly talk about myself and my accomplishments, but I also make an effort to show interest in others occasionally.

4 - I mostly talk about myself and my accomplishments, and I rarely show interest in others.

5 - I always talk about myself and my accomplishments, and I never show interest in others.

Q2. Do you expect special treatment from others and get upset when you don't receive it?

Score: _____

0 - I don't expect special treatment and am not upset when I don't receive it.

1 - I don't expect special treatment, but I may feel a little disappointed when I don't receive it.

2 - I expect special treatment occasionally, and I may feel upset or annoyed when I don't receive it.

3 - I often expect special treatment, and I get upset or annoyed when I don't receive it.

4 - I almost always expect special treatment, and I get very upset or angry when I don't receive it.

5 - I always expect special treatment, and I get extremely upset or angry when I don't receive it.

Q3. Do you have an over-inflated sense of your own importance or abilities?

Score: _____

0 – I have a realistic sense of my own importance and abilities.

1 - I may have some moments of over-inflation, but overall, I have a realistic sense of my own importance and abilities.

2 – I have some over-inflation of my own importance and abilities, but I'm aware of it and try to keep it in check.

3 – I have a consistently over-inflated sense of my own importance and abilities, but I'm aware of it and try to keep it in check.

4 – I have a consistently over-inflated sense of my own importance and abilities, and I'm not always aware of it.

5 – I have a consistently over-inflated sense of my importance and abilities, and I'm not aware of it at all.

Q4. Do you take advantage of others to get what you want?

Score: _____

0 - I never take advantage of others to get what I want.

1 - I rarely take advantage of others to get what I want.

2 - I sometimes take advantage of others to get what I want.

3 - I often take advantage of others to get what I want.

4 - I almost always take advantage of others to get what I want.

5 - I always take advantage of others to get what I want.

Q5. Do you often lack empathy for the feelings and experiences of others?

Score: _____

0 – I have a high level of empathy and regularly consider the feelings and experiences of others.

1 – I have a good level of empathy and often consider the feelings and experiences of others.

2 – I have some empathy, but I don't always consider the feelings and experiences of others.

3 – I have a limited amount of empathy and don't often consider the feelings and experiences of others.

4 – I have a very limited amount of empathy and rarely consider the feelings and experiences of others.

5 – I have no empathy and never consider the feelings and experiences of others.

Q6. Do you have difficulty being vulnerable or admitting when you're wrong?

Score: _____

0 - I'm very comfortable being vulnerable and openly admitting I'm wrong. I understand that vulnerability and mistakes are a natural part of being human, and I'm not afraid to show that side of myself to others.

1 - I'm generally comfortable being vulnerable and admitting when I'm wrong, but there may be certain situations where I struggle with it.

2 - I'm somewhat uncomfortable with being vulnerable and admitting when I'm wrong, but I can do it if necessary.

3 - I'm generally uncomfortable with being vulnerable and admitting when I'm wrong, and I try to avoid it whenever possible.

4 - I'm very uncomfortable with being vulnerable and admitting when I'm wrong, and I do anything I can to avoid it.

5 - I can't be vulnerable or admit when I'm wrong, and I become defensive or deny it even when the evidence is clear.

Q7. Do you frequently disregard rules and regulations, particularly if they don't align with your desires or beliefs?

Score: _____

0 - I always follow the rules and regulations, even if they don't align with my desires or beliefs.

1 - I generally follow the rules and regulations, but there may be occasional exceptions if I feel strongly about something.

2 - I often follow the rules and regulations, but I may bend or break them if it suits my own needs or desires.

3 - I frequently disregard rules and regulations, and I will break them if it suits my own needs or desires.

4 - I consistently disregard rules and regulations, and I have little regard for the consequences of breaking them.

5 - I completely disregard rules and regulations and actively seek opportunities to break them.

Q8. Do you have difficulty understanding and considering the perspective of others, particularly if it conflicts with your own?

Score: _____

0 - I'm very good at understanding and considering the perspective of others, even if it conflicts with my own.

1 - I'm generally good at understanding and considering the perspective of others, but there may be some situations where I struggle with it.

2 - I'm somewhat able to understand and consider the perspective of others, but it can be difficult for me to do so, especially if it conflicts with my own.

3 – I have a limited ability to understand and consider the perspective of others, and I tend to prioritize my perspective over theirs.

4 – I have a very limited ability to understand and consider the perspective of others, and I'm resistant to hearing their perspective if it conflicts with my own.

5 - I'm completely unable to understand or consider the perspective of others, and I become defensive or dismissive when confronted with a different viewpoint.

Q9. Do you tend to blame others for your problems or mistakes?

Score: _____

0 - No, I take responsibility for my actions and mistakes.

1 - Sometimes, depending on the situation and my mood.

2 - I may blame others occasionally, but I try to take ownership of my mistakes.

3 - I often blame others for my problems and may deflect criticism or feedback.

4 - I always blame others for my problems and rarely take responsibility for my actions.

5 - I believe that I'm never at fault for anything and that others are always to blame.

Q10. Do you often interrupt others when they are speaking?

Score: _____

0 - No, I rarely interrupt others and try to listen actively.

1 - Sometimes, if I'm excited or passionate about the topic.

2 - I interrupt others occasionally, but I try to be aware of it and apologize.

3 - I frequently interrupt others and may dominate the conversation.

4 - I always interrupt others and may talk over them or dismiss their ideas.

5 - I believe my opinions and ideas are the only ones that matter, so I constantly interrupt others.

TOTAL SCORE: _____

What does the total score mean?

- Scores of 10 or less mean that the range is good to average.

- If your score is between 10 and 17, you're a bit too self-centered in how you act. If you pay a little more interest to your more self-centered habits, you might be able to lower that score by a lot with only a little bit of work.

- If you get a score of 18 or more, it means you have a lot of narcissistic habits that probably won't help you. It might be time to change some big habits!

- If you get a score of 24 or more, you have many problems with being self-centered. We hope you're ready to make a serious effort to grow as a person.

If the results of this quiz make you feel uncomfortable, know that it's not a test for narcissism. Instead of using scoring systems that have been proven by science, these tests use general patterns to figure out what the scores mean. These tests aim not to diagnose patients but to give them a fair warning.

To get a definite diagnosis, tests need to be done by mental health professionals. A few diagnostic tests that may be used to diagnose NPD are:

1. Narcissistic Personality Inventory (NPI): This self-report questionnaire measures narcissistic traits. It consists of 40 items that individuals rate on a scale of 0 to 4 based on how well the item describes them. The NPI is widely used in research and is a reliable measure of narcissistic traits.

2. Diagnostic and Statistical Manual of Mental Disorders (DSM-5): This manual is used by mental health experts to diagnose mental health conditions. It includes specific criteria that must be met to diagnose NPD. The DSM-5 criteria for NPD include an exaggerated sense of haughtiness, a need for admiration, and a lack of empathy, among other symptoms.

3. Structured Clinical Interview for DSM-5 Personality Disorders (SCID-5-PD): This is a semi-structured interview used to assess for personality disorders, including NPD. It consists of questions and prompts designed to elicit information about an individual's personality and behavior. The SCID-5-PD is administered by a mental health professional and requires a high level of training to use accurately.

4. Millon Clinical Multiaxial Inventory-III (MCMI-III): This self-report questionnaire assesses personality disorders, including NPD. It consists of 175 items that individuals rate on a scale of 0 to 4 based on how well the item describes them. The MCMI-III is widely used in research and is a reliable measure of narcissistic traits.

It's important to note that these tests should be administered by a qualified mental health professional and should not be used for self-diagnosis. A mental health professional is the only person who could tell if someone has NPD. Psychologists, psychiatrists, or other mental health professionals diagnose NPD after speaking with the patient and reviewing their medical history. Even a professional in mental health might not always be able to spot NPD as easily as they would like and that's because people with NPD rarely go to therapists and if they do, they might not talk openly about their thoughts.

In addition to the diagnostic tests administered, the therapist will keep an eye on and measure the following:

• The person's characteristics

• The person's behavior in the real world (relationships, jobs, etc.)

- The person's sense of identity

- The person's self-esteem and how it changes over time

- The person's empathy level

The mental health professional will try to find at least five signs of NPD. If they do, they'll be able to determine what's wrong and suggest the right treatment.

Even though teens may show signs of the disorder early on, NPD is usually diagnosed when the person is an adult. Physical and mental growth is still going on in children and teenagers. Changes in personality that keep occurring at a young age might make it hard to see long-term behavior patterns. If a person is diagnosed with NPD when they're a teen, it's because they've been acting the same way for more than a year.

How NPD is diagnosed has been the subject of some debate. This is mostly because many mental health professionals have focused on the most obvious social behaviors of people with NPD and not enough on their inner struggles, vulnerabilities, and challenges. This can make people judge instead of trying to understand.

So far, we've discussed the main characteristics of narcissism and how to diagnose it. We've seen that narcissists often exhibit an over-inflated sense of importance, a lack of empathy, and a tendency to blame others for their mistakes. We also know that narcissism can emerge due to multiple factors, including environmental and genetic factors, but the most common one is childhood trauma which can be easily identified. Childhood trauma can lead to the development of negative coping mechanisms and an unhealthy sense of self.

In the next chapter, we will delve deeper into childhood trauma and how it can impact an individual's development. We'll also discuss strategies for overcoming childhood trauma and working towards healing and personal growth. We'll explore the different therapeutic approaches that can provide relief and healing. Moreover, we'll examine how to support someone struggling with the effects of childhood trauma and the importance of self-care to prevent future trauma. Additionally, we'll look at the importance of developing healthy coping strategies that can be used to manage stress and difficult emotions. Finally, we'll talk about the benefits of seeking professional help and the treatment options available. By knowing these steps, we can create a plan of action to help ourselves or our loved ones who're dealing with childhood trauma.

Chapter 4:
How to Overcome Childhood Emotional Neglect

C hildhood emotional neglect is child abuse in which a parent or caregiver fails to offer the emotional support and guidance a child requires to develop. Examples of this are failure to provide comfort or affection, to respond effectively to a kid's emotional needs, or to provide a safe and stable environment for the child to grow and develop.

Emotional neglect can manifest itself in a variety of ways during childhood. Here are a few examples:

- Failure to provide emotional support: A parent or caregiver may be emotionally unavailable to a kid or fail to respond to the child's emotional needs in a timely or suitable manner. When a parent is upset, they may not give their child a hug or verbal comfort or dismiss the youngster's sentiments when they express them.

  Failure to provide sufficient advice and structure: A parent or caregiver may fail to provide appropriate guidance and structure to the kid, making it difficult for the youngster to feel safe and comfortable. A parent, for example, may fail to establish clear standards or boundaries or be inconsistent in enforcing rules in the home.

- Failure to offer a stable environment: A parent or caregiver may fail to provide a stable and safe environment for their child, making it difficult for the child to feel secure.

Several variables can cause emotional neglect, and parents may ignore their children for various reasons. Among the possible causes are:

- Mental health issues: A parent or caregiver who suffers from depression, anxiety, or substance misuse may find it difficult to provide emotional support and direction to their child.

- Stress and burnout: A parent or caregiver may be stressed out owing to financial or relationship problems, work-related issues, or other stressors.

- A parent or caregiver may lack the knowledge or abilities required to provide proper emotional support and guidance to a kid.

- Socioeconomic status: In some situations, a parent or caregiver may not have access to the resources needed to provide proper emotional support and guidance to a kid, such as schooling, stable housing, and access to mental health treatments.

Most parents are well-intentioned, and they do their best. Some may have endured emotional neglect as youngsters and may not have much to offer emotionally. Some parenting approaches and behaviors, however, lead to emotional neglect.

- Authoritarian parents expect their children to obey the rules and have little time or interest in listening to their children's feelings and needs. Children reared by an authoritarian parent may revolt against authority as adults or become docile.

- Permissive parents take a laissez-faire approach and may leave their children to fend for themselves. Children raised by permissive parents may struggle to create boundaries and limitations for themselves as adults.

- Narcissistic parents believe the world revolves around them. It's usually all about the parents' needs rather than the children's needs. These children may have difficulties identifying and meeting their needs as adults. They may even believe they don't deserve to have their basic needs satisfied.

- Parents who're perfectionists feel their children can always achieve more or better. These parents could object if their child comes home with a report card with all As and one B. Children raised by such parents may become perfectionists with impossibly high standards for themselves, resulting in anxiety over never being good enough.

- Absent parents might be taken out of a child's life for various reasons, including death, illness, divorce, working long hours, or regular business travel. A child raised by absent parents must largely raise themselves and, if older, may raise their younger siblings. These youngsters are often overly responsible, which can carry over into adulthood. As children, they appear to be small grownups burdened with concern for their families.

It's crucial to highlight that emotional neglect may occur in any household, regardless of socioeconomic class, race, religion, or ethnicity. Any parent can struggle to provide emotional support and guidance to their child at some point due to personal circumstances.

Children who're emotionally neglected may show signs in several ways. Some possible indicators of emotional neglect in a child include:

- Behavioral issues: Children who're emotionally neglected may demonstrate several behavioral issues, including anger, defiance, and acting out. They may also be withdrawn, indifferent, or struggle to obey norms and directions.

- Emotional control difficulties: Children who've experienced emotional neglect may have trouble managing their emotions. They may be easily agitated, experience abrupt mood shifts, or have difficulty settling down.

- Poor self-esteem: Children who've experienced emotional neglect may have low self-esteem, manifesting as negative self-talk or lacking confidence in their talents.

- Relationship difficulties: Children who've experienced emotional neglect may have trouble building relationships with others. They may be hesitant to establish acquaintances or have difficulty forming close emotional connections with others.

- Academic difficulties: Children who've experienced emotional neglect may struggle in school because they have difficulty focusing and paying attention.

- Lack of appropriate emotional expression: Children who're emotionally neglected may exhibit little or no emotional expression or may be unable to identify or communicate their emotions.

Not all sufferers of childhood emotional abuse will exhibit all of these symptoms, and some children may be more resilient than others. However, if a child exhibits many indicators of emotional neglect over a long period, it may indicate that they suffer from emotional neglect. Furthermore, because children can't always express their emotions verbally, studying their behavior and emotional states over time may provide a clearer picture of their emotional neglect.

Emotional neglect can have substantial short and long-term consequences for a child's development, resulting in anxiety, depression, and trouble building healthy relationships later in life. However, it's frequently disregarded in psychology since it's often silent and difficult to detect. There are often no apparent indications, as opposed to physical neglect or abuse, which can be seen in bruises or children arriving at school famished. More importantly, a child usually doesn't realize they're being emotionally ignored until the youngster is an adult. As a result, there aren't as many statistics as possible. According to one meta-study, 184 out of every 1000 children have been emotionally abused. Emotional neglect in childhood increases the likelihood of anxiety disorders as a teen or adult.

Emotional neglect can have the following effects on children:

- Emotional and mental health issues: Children who've experienced emotional neglect are more likely to develop emotional and mental health issues such as anxiety, sadness, and post-traumatic stress disorder (PTSD). They may struggle with mood regulation, stress management, and building healthy relationships.

- Difficulties trusting others: Children who've experienced emotional neglect may struggle to trust others, making it difficult to build healthy connections later in life. They may be more withdrawn or have difficulty trusting.

- Difficulties understanding and expressing emotions: Children who've experienced emotional neglect may struggle to understand and express their feelings and emotions, as well as the emotions of others. They may not have been trained to recognize and express emotions effectively.

- Behavioral issues: Children who're emotionally neglected may demonstrate a variety of behavioral issues, including anger, defiance, and acting out. These activities could be a way for them to communicate their emotional pain and seek attention.

- Academic difficulties: Children who've experienced emotional neglect may have difficulty focusing and paying attention in school owing to emotional and mental health issues such as anxiety or sadness.

- Difficulties in building healthy relationships: Children who've experienced emotional neglect may struggle later in life to form healthy relationships because they have difficulty trusting others and expressing their emotions appropriately.

It's vital to highlight that emotional neglect can exacerbate other forms of abuse and neglect, such as physical, sexual, and financial neglect. It's also worth noting that not all children will experience all of these consequences, and some may be more resilient than others.

Children who're emotionally neglected may not receive the direction, comfort, and validation they require to learn how to cope with life's regular ups and downs and process and understand their feelings. As they get older, they may be more vulnerable to mental disturbances. They may have self-esteem, self-worth, self-compassion issues, and problems understanding and expressing their feelings. They may also struggle to build healthy connections and trust people, both of which can contribute to feelings of emotional anguish. Furthermore, emotional neglect can have a compounding impact, which frequently coexists with other forms of abuse or neglect, such as physical, sexual, or environmental neglect, resulting in more severe and long-lasting emotional suffering.

Emotional distress is a condition of psychological and emotional suffering characterized by acute discomforts, such as anxiety, grief, and rage. Several factors, including tough life events, trauma, and mental health issues, can cause emotional distress. Emotional discomfort can cause various physical, emotional, and behavioral symptoms, interfering with a person's ability to function in daily life.

Examples of emotional distress symptoms include:

- Feelings of despair, pessimism, or worthlessness that persist
- Panic or anxiety attacks
- Loss of interest or enjoyment in activities
- Irritation, rage, or hostility
- Sleeping difficulties or excessive sleep
- Concentration issues
- Fatigue or a lack of energy
- Headaches, stomachaches, and muscle tension are examples of physical symptoms.
- Appetite or weight changes
- Difficulties making decisions or solving problems
- Self-destructive behavior like substance abuse or self-harm
- Senses of shame or guilt

Emotional distress can range in severity from moderate and transient to severe and chronic. It's an important and normal component of the human experience, and learning to understand and handle our emotions can provide a chance for personal growth and healing. However, when emotional distress becomes protracted and chronic, it may suggest the need for professional assistance, and it's critical to seek assistance to enhance and preserve our emotional well-being.

Childhood emotional neglect (CEN) can have substantial and long-term consequences for a person's emotional and mental health as an adult, as well as their relationships and overall well-being. CEN can impact adults in a variety of ways, including:

- Adults who experienced CEN as children may be more likely to develop emotional and mental health issues, such as anxiety, depression, and difficulty managing emotions. They may have issues with their self-esteem, self-worth, and self-identity.

- Difficult internal emotions and feelings: Adults with CEN frequently experience a sense of "numbing out" or being cut off from their emotions. Feeling as if something is missing but not knowing what it is. Feeling hollow on the inside.

- Difficulty understanding and expressing emotions: Adults who were exposed to CEN as children may struggle to understand and express their feelings as well as the emotions of others. They may be oblivious to their emotional needs and have difficulty empathizing with others.

- Difficulties with relationships: Adults who experienced CEN as children may struggle with sexual and platonic relationships. They may struggle to trust others and form intimate emotional connections with others. They may also have boundary issues, resulting in toxic or unstable relationships.

- Difficulties with self-care and self-compassion: Adults exposed to CEN as children may struggle with self-care and self-compassion. They may be prone to self-sacrifice, self-criticism, and self-doubt and struggle to establish limits and assert themselves.

- Difficulties at work: Adults who had CEN as children may struggle to find purpose in their professions. They may be less self-assured, less resilient to stress, and less able to trust or form relationships with coworkers.

It's crucial to emphasize that these are broad impacts, and people will react differently. Some people may be more impacted than others, and not everyone who has CEN will experience all of these symptoms. However, it's very usual for people to have a combination of these consequences, depending on how they affect their lives and perceive themselves.

It's also worth noting that CEN is sometimes overlooked by adults who experienced it as children, and they may fail to associate some of their issues and problems with the lack of emotional care they received as children. Therapy, self-help, and personal development can aid in recognizing and treating the impact of CEN.

Recognizing the indicators of childhood emotional neglect (CEN) can be difficult since it's frequently a subtle kind of abuse, and the person may not associate their issues and problems with a lack of emotional care as a child. However, you should be aware of several frequent signs and symptoms of CEN in your behavior.

- Difficulty understanding and expressing emotions: If you have difficulty understanding and expressing your feelings or comprehending the emotions of others, you may have experienced CEN.

- Difficulty creating healthy connections: If you're having difficulty forming romantic and platonic relationships, this could be a symptom of CEN.

- Emotional and mental health issues: If you battle mental health issues like anxiety, depression, or difficulties controlling emotions, it could be a symptom of CEN.

- Difficulties with self-care and self-compassion: If you find it difficult to care for yourself emotionally or physically, or if you have difficulty being compassionate, you may have CEN.

- Difficulty at work: If you struggle to trust or create relationships with colleagues and coworkers, you may have CEN.

- Difficulty with personal boundaries: If you find it difficult to set personal boundaries, express yourself, or say no, this could be a symptom of CEN.

Childhood emotional neglect is a challenging diagnosis since it's frequently not acknowledged by the person who has experienced it and can be a subtle type of abuse. However, skilled therapists or counselors can employ various strategies to identify and diagnose CEN. Among these techniques are:

- Self-report measures, such as questionnaires or interviews, may be used by therapists to acquire information on a person's early experiences and current emotional and mental health. These assessments can aid in identifying patterns of emotional neglect and provide a comprehensive picture of a person's experience.

- A therapist or counselor may observe a person's behavior and communication during therapy sessions. They may search for indicators of difficulty understanding or expressing emotions, self-worth issues, and difficulties building healthy relationships.

A therapist may ask a person to explain their childhood experiences, particularly the emotional milieu in which they grew up and their relationship with their parents or caregivers. They may search for signs of neglect and a lack of emotional support. A therapist may also assess a person's current functioning, including their emotional and mental health, relationships, and overall well-being. They may seek patterns of problems that can be traced back to emotional neglect in childhood.

While CEN can contribute to numerous mental and emotional difficulties, other factors such as genetics, trauma, and environment can also play a role. So, before making a diagnosis, a therapist will also consider those factors. CEN can also be diagnosed with other types of abuse or neglect, including physical and sexual abuse.

It's also worth noting that CEN can be difficult to spot and diagnose, and the identification procedure might be lengthy. A therapist will work closely with the individual to help them comprehend and process their experience and identify any harmful patterns or behaviors that arise from their childhood emotional neglect.

However, the good news is that the effects of CEN can be treated and recovered with the support of a qualified therapist or counselor and self-help approaches.

1. Therapist-assisted treatments:

- Therapy: Therapy is a helpful method of dealing with the impacts of CEN. A therapist can help a person comprehend their experiences and feelings and create coping methods to deal with the negative impacts of CEN. Therapy can also assist a person in identifying and changing negative patterns of behavior and thought that CEN had caused. Cognitive behavioral therapy (CBT), eye movement desensitization and reprocessing (EMDR), and family systems therapy may be beneficial.

- Medication: Medication may be used in conjunction with therapy to treat CEN symptoms. Antidepressants, for example, may be used to treat symptoms of sadness and anxiety, while anti-anxiety medication may treat anxiety symptoms.

2. Dealing with CEN on a personal level:

So, what should you do if you felt emotionally ignored as a child? Here are some pointers:

- Consider the emotional neglect in your family and how it has affected you:

  This isn't as simple as it appears. For example, it's critical to determine whether it was simply one parent or both. Did your parents neglect your feelings because they were dealing with their problems? Because they were self-centered and only concerned about themselves? Or were they simply unaware of the significance of emotions? Were you active or passive in your emotional neglect, rude or nice? How did it impact you as a child, and how does it affect you now? Understanding your CEN deeply can help you stop blaming and humiliating yourself and will give your experience more weight.

- Recognize that your feelings are blocked but that they're still present and waiting for you:

  Your child's brain insulated you from your sensations by erecting barriers, but it couldn't remove them. You can still reach them right now. Accepting that they exist can assist you in learning how to listen to, use, and regulate them.

- Consider your feelings:

  This is the most beneficial thing you can do to manage your CEN. It's a way to defy what your parents taught you, to start respecting your feelings, and to reach across the wall to the richness, color, and connection that lie on the other side: your emotions. You can begin to use them the way they were intended if you pay attention to how you feel.

- Taking the time to face negative emotions will help you deal with them more effectively:

  Learning to sit with strong or painful emotions is one of the most important early steps in developing all emotional abilities. If you sit with your negative emotions, you'll regain control of yourself.

- Maintain a running list of your likes and dislikes:

  Pay close attention and keep things in mind as you go about your day. Write down anything you can think of that you enjoy or dislike. You can make yourself happier if you know these facts about yourself.

- Have and demonstrate compassion for oneself:

  You probably treat others far better than yourself if you have CEN. As a human being, remember that you have the same rights as everyone else. You'll fail because you'll make mistakes and poor decisions. And you shouldn't be harsher on yourself than you would be on a loved one who did the same thing. Self-compassion will assist you in loving yourself more.

- Pay attention to how you feel in your body when you're furious:

  Anger is the one emotion that'll destroy you if you don't let it out and deal with it. When you become conscious of your anger, it calms you down and gives you more power.

- Read a book about determination:

  When you recognize your anger, the next stage is learning to assert yourself. Being assertive is a technique for ensuring that others understand what you want, need, and feel. People will like you more if you learn to be more forceful.

- Share your CEN experience with someone close to you:

  When you tell others about your CEN experience, you feel you own it and take it seriously. You'll feel less burdened and alone if you tell someone about your CEN.

- Consider how CEN impacts your most critical connections:

  Has the emotional maltreatment you endured as a child manifested itself in your marriage? Have you changed the way you've raised your children? Do your parents make you feel uncomfortable? Looking for CEN's effects on the people you care about will help you get closer to them.

Keep in mind that Rome wasn't built in a day! This is how it operates. When you cut your knee, clean it and expose it to sunlight. The same holds when you hurt someone's feelings. Dare to pull the wound out of hiding, allowing light and air to enter it, and you'll begin to feel better. It's crucial to recognize that recovery and healing take time, are unique to each individual, and that everyone has distinct requirements and ways that work best for them. It's critical to be patient and compassionate with yourself and to avoid comparing your progress to that of others. Remember that healing and recovery are possible and that seeking professional assistance and self-help methods can improve your emotional and mental well-being.

In conclusion, CEN can significantly impact a person's life, especially for those prone to narcissism. CEN can cause various emotional and mental health issues, including anxiety, despair, and difficulties controlling emotions. It can also make it difficult to build good relationships, trust others, and comprehend and express one's emotions. CEN may be especially damaging to narcissists, who struggle to comprehend and attend to their emotional needs and rely significantly on external validation and adulation.

CEN recovery is attainable with professional counseling, self-awareness, self-care, and the support of others. Healing the inner child is critical in recovery because it allows one to comprehend and address unmet emotional needs from the past and build healthier methods of coping and interacting with others. You'll find out more about your inner child and how to heal it in the next chapter.

Chapter 5:
Healing Your Inner Child

T he "inner child" refers to a person's emotional and psychological aspects associated with childhood experiences and memories. It's the part of our personality and self that contains emotions, behaviors, and beliefs that were formed in childhood and continue to influence a person's thoughts, feelings, and actions in adulthood. We all have an inner child within ourselves that has been with us ever since conception, in utero, childhood, and all the years in which we were young and developing into our tender selves. It's common for the inner child to recall good experiences and childhood fears, traumas, neglect, or significant losses.

We can start to notice the internal patterns that have left us a subconscious "breadcrumb trail" as we start to delve into our inner world when we begin to pinpoint the exact event that tugs at us. The inner child exists within each of us. The inner child is a part of you that picks up messages before it can fully process them (mentally and emotionally). It's often associated with the idea that unresolved emotional issues from childhood can affect a person's behavior and emotional well-being in adulthood. Healing the inner child involves working through unresolved emotional issues and unprocessed traumas to achieve greater emotional balance and well-being in adulthood.

A damaged or wounded inner child can be caused by a variety of factors, including:

- Trauma: Experiencing traumatic events in childhood, such as physical, emotional, or sexual abuse, neglect, or abandonment, can lead to a damaged or wounded inner child.

- Neglect: A lack of emotional, physical, or mental support from caregivers can also lead to a damaged or wounded inner child.

- Unhealthy family dynamics: Growing up in a dysfunctional family, such as chronic conflict, verbal or physical abuse, or addiction, can also contribute to a damaged or wounded inner child.

- Unmet needs: When a child's emotional, psychological, or physical needs are not met, this can lead to a damaged or wounded inner child.

- Unrealistic expectations or harsh criticism from parents, teachers, or other important adults in their life.

Not all of the above factors will damage the inner child of everyone. The impact depends on the individual and the severity of the experiences. Sometimes, an accumulation of small negative experiences can lead to a damaged inner child, just as a single big traumatic event can.

It's important to know that these experiences can create limiting beliefs, low self-esteem, fear, trust issues, and other emotional struggles that can affect a person's relationships and ability to cope with stress, leading to emotional and psychological problems in adulthood.

From birth until the age of seven, we have an 'ego-centric' view of the world - we believe everything that happens in our immediate environment is somehow linked to us or caused by us. This isn't a rational or logical stage, yet many core ideas about the world are formed before seven. For instance, if you have a parent with depression, your inner child might become triggered if your romantic partner becomes depressed. If a child's parents are divorcing, they might blame themselves and think it's because they're naughty rather than understanding that the grownups are having relationship problems. A trigger could be anything, from a critical boss who unconsciously reminds you of a fault-finding parent to feeling socially anxious in a group because you were bullied at school. It could also be small on the surface, causing you to wonder why you're 'overreacting,' but this is because things that seem trivial to your adult self can be huge to your inner child.

"Our childhood becomes the filter through which all new experiences must pass," says John Bradshaw, author of *Home Coming*. This explains why some people choose the same kind of bad relationship, feel like their lives are a series of traumas they've already been through, and why so many of us don't learn from our mistakes.

Not all of us had unfortunate childhoods, but we were hurt in some way when our needs weren't met in our childhood. Even if your family life was mostly happy, no one's childhood is free of confusion, disappointment, or sadness. Some of those problems may have been solved, but others may still be bothering you without you realizing it. As we get older, we lose touch with our inner child's needs, pains, hopes, and dreams, often ignoring them so we can be what society says we should be. When we're young, we don't care if something is real. Reality and make-believe blend like carefree watercolors. Then, one day, we stop playing altogether. We don't pay enough attention to our inner child so that we have room for our adult lives and the many expectations we have to meet to be accepted.

Some signs and symptoms that may indicate that a person's inner child is wounded include:

- Difficulty trusting others or forming close relationships
- Difficulty managing emotions, like feeling overwhelmed by negative emotions
- Difficulty setting boundaries
- Chronic feelings of insecurity, shame, or inadequacy
- Difficulty having fun or engaging in activities that bring joy
- Difficulty feeling safe and secure
- Difficulty feeling emotionally connected to others
- Difficulty expressing emotions or needs
- Difficulty feeling deserving of love and happiness
- Difficulty feeling in control of one's life

It's important to note that having one or more of these warning signs doesn't necessarily mean a person's inner child is wounded. Some of these issues can be caused by other factors, such as life experiences or personal circumstances. However, if a person is experiencing a number of these symptoms, it may be worth exploring the possibility that their inner child is wounded and seeking professional help.

If individuals don't take the time to heal their inner child, they may experience difficulties in their daily life, relationships, and emotional well-being. This can include difficulties forming and maintaining healthy relationships, managing emotions, setting boundaries, and achieving personal goals. Additionally, individuals may struggle with trust issues, insecurity, inadequacy, and difficulties feeling safe and emotionally connected to others. They may also find it difficult to feel deserving of love and happiness, feel in control of their life, or find fulfillment and satisfaction in life. Furthermore, not healing the inner child can also make it harder to deal with stress or trauma healthily, leaving the person stuck in a difficult cycle of negative thoughts and emotions that can be hard to break out of. All these may lead to a compromise in overall well-being and mental and emotional health.

Dr. Venetia Leonidaki says, "From a young age on, we have to find a balance between our emotional needs and the demands or limits that other people put on us." Parents, teachers, and later partners, employers, and children expect us to be responsible, in control of our feelings, logical and follow social norms. Since we always have to balance our needs with pressures from the outside world, we often repress and cut ourselves off from our inner child.

Connecting with your inner child can be a powerful way to gain insight into your emotions, beliefs, and behaviors and begin healing past wounds. Here are a few approaches you can utilize to begin connecting with your inner child:

- Accept: Take responsibility for the pain you experienced as a child and accept it.

- Pay attention: When you open the door to your inner child, pay attention to the feelings you experience. How do you feel when angry, rejected, vulnerable, guilty, or anxious? Is there anything in your adult life or relationship that triggers these feelings?

- Let's talk: If you want to connect with your inner child, consider writing a letter to them. What is your inner child feeling? "What can I do to help you?" and "How can I help you?" Your inner child can feel safe and secure if you work at it.

- Meditation or visualization: Set aside some quiet time to sit or lie in a comfortable place, close your eyes, and visualize yourself as a child. Imagine yourself sitting in a room with your inner child and spending some time getting to know them.

- Journaling: Write down any memories, feelings, or thoughts that come to mind when you remember your childhood. This can be an effective way to access and process emotions connected to your inner child.

- Art: Use art to express feelings or emotions that are connected to your inner child. This can include drawing, painting, or sculpting, and it can be a way to connect with the childlike, intuitive, and imaginative part of yourself.

- Play like a child: Allow yourself to engage in activities and hobbies that bring you joy and a sense of playfulness. As adults, we often forget the importance of play and fun. However, it's vital for healing the inner child.

- Therapy: Seek a therapist or counselor trained in inner child issues. They can help you understand and work through the emotions, beliefs, and behaviors connected to your inner child.

Remember, connecting with your inner child is a personal and unique process. You may need to try different approaches and see what works for you. It's important to be patient and kind with yourself as you explore and connect with your inner child.

During inner child healing, a person works through unresolved emotional issues and unprocessed traumas from childhood to achieve greater emotional balance and well-being in adulthood. The process of inner child healing involves six steps:

1. Acknowledging the inner child: Recognizing the existence of an inner child and the importance of addressing any unresolved emotional issues or traumas that may be impacting your emotional well-being.

2. Accessing the inner child: Finding ways to connect with the childlike aspect of yourself, such as through meditation, visualization, journaling, art, play, and therapy.

3. Identifying and expressing emotions: Identifying the emotions connected to your inner child and learning healthy ways to express and process those emotions.

4. Challenging limiting beliefs and reprogramming: Examining the negative beliefs and thought patterns formed due to childhood experiences and learning to challenge and change them.

5. Building a supportive inner environment: Creating a supportive inner environment by developing self-compassion, self-love, and self-care and learning to create healthy boundaries and relationships.

6. Letting go: Releasing past traumas and negative experiences and learning to forgive others and yourself.

Start to parent yourself again. Re-parenting is when you take on the role of a parent or caretaker and give the emotional support you may have needed as a child or as you grew up. Re-parenting is based on the connection with that inner self.

If we had a bad childhood or didn't get enough help, we may have had to separate from our true selves and make a fake one to survive and get through it. Our inner child lives in the part of us that feels and experiences, and our inner adult lives in the part of us that thinks and makes decisions. The part of us that is most innocent and carefree is our inner child. Our inner adult, on the other hand, is the part of us that is out in the world and doing things. If you had a hard childhood, you might have had to cut yourself off from your inner self because the feelings and emotions were too much.

So, re-parenting is the process of being open, setting an intention to learn about this inner self that we weren't able to grow when we were younger, and attaching or connecting this inner child with the inner self that we need to fix.

It might seem like a lot, but think about how you would act and talk to a child you adopted. You wouldn't say anything hurtful to a child, would you? You would never embarrass a child, but we always do it to ourselves. Think of your inner child as the child you just took in. You won't be mean to that child. You'll love and take care of it, so you need to have this kind of love and care in you.

When we separate from our inner child because we're looking for validation from the outside, we also need to find out what we're good at and worth. Separating from our inner child could be because we didn't have good, caring caregivers when we were young who validated us the right way or because we're only valued for our talents or skills. We should try to figure out what our true worth is and know that we're important just because we're alive and a person, and we have to tell ourselves and our inner selves that over and over again. Moreover, when we've been disconnected from our internal environment for a while, it can be scary to go back in, so we may connect with it for a while and then disconnect, but in the end, we need to practice staying connected within this internal environment not just when we're meditating, not just when we're closing our eyes, but being connected at all times so that we can travel and grow consciously.

Be aware of when you're blaming yourself. It's easy to do and can happen quickly, but we can't be loving parents if we're always shaming ourselves. We need to change the story, recognize the shameful thoughts that come up and fight them, and be loving parents.

Re-parenting is a spiritual process that requires us to break down the walls of the ego, call ourselves forward, and let the soul or a higher power guide us through it. We also have to be ready to face some of the hardest emotions we've been avoiding, but it's worth it because it heals depression, anxiety, and childhood traumas. This helps us love ourselves in the long run because it fills our emptiness.

In my opinion, healing the inner child can be an emotionally challenging process. Be patient and have realistic expectations. Seeking guidance from a therapist or counselor trained in working with inner child issues can greatly help this journey. Remember that healing the inner child is a process that can take time and patience and that the journey may involve exploring old wounds and painful memories. Inner child healing isn't a one-time event; it's an ongoing process that requires continuous work and may take time, but with commitment and dedication, a person can see positive changes in their emotions, relationships, and overall well-being.

Becoming curious about yourself is one of the first signs that you're healing your inner child. Identifying core childhood wounds behind triggers can also help heal inner child wounds. Maintaining self-trust between the present-day self and inner child is a key sign of inner child healing. Making time for play signifies that you're healing your inner child. Inner child healing allows for authentic self-expression. Feeling free and experiencing less struggle in areas are telltale signs you've been doing inner child work. The reason is that the inner child's needs differ from the adult's needs.

The effects of inner child work can spill over into your relationships. Your mood will, of course, change, but the fluctuations won't be as extreme as before. You'll feel less anxious and generally calmer, improving sleep and making you less preoccupied during social interactions.

Here are a few other signs that your inner child may be healing:

- Improved emotional regulation: You may find that you can better manage your emotions and feel more balanced overall.

- Better relationships: You may start to notice that your relationships are improving and that you feel more connected to others.

- Increased self-awareness: You may become more aware of your thoughts, feelings, and behaviors, which can help you make positive changes.

- Increased self-compassion: You may find that you're less critical of yourself and have more self-compassion.

- Increased trust: Trusting others and yourself may become easier.

- Sense of peace: You may feel a sense of peace and greater happiness and fulfillment in life.

- Feeling of control: You may feel like you have greater control over your life and can better set and maintain healthy boundaries.

Again, it's important to remember that healing the inner child is a process, and you may experience setbacks or challenges. It's essential to be kind and compassionate with yourself as you continue to work through the process of inner child healing.

I'd like to give you a sneak peek at what you'll be reading about in the upcoming chapters; shadow self. A shadow self refers to the parts of a person's psyche that they're unaware of or don't want to accept. It can include negative traits, fears, and repressed emotions. These parts of the self may come to light through dreams or during therapy.

It's often thought of as the "dark side" of a person's personality. Understanding and accepting the shadow self is important to have a healthy and well-rounded sense of self.

Healing the inner child can have a direct impact on our shadow self in several ways:

- Greater self-awareness: As we work to heal the inner child, we become more aware of the emotions, beliefs, and behaviors connected to our childhood experiences. This increased self-awareness allows us to understand how our past experiences impact our present and to make positive changes in our thoughts, behaviors, and emotions.

- Processing and releasing repressed emotions: As we work to heal the inner child, we may process and release repressed emotions such as fear, shame, guilt, anger, and sadness. As these emotions are processed and released, they're no longer held in the shadow self, leading to a greater sense of emotional balance and well-being.

- Challenge limiting beliefs and negative thought patterns: Inner child healing can help us challenge the limiting beliefs and negative thought patterns formed due to childhood experiences. This can help reduce the shadow self's influence on our thoughts, feelings, and behaviors.

- Building a more supportive inner environment: As we work to heal the inner child, we can develop self-compassion, self-love, and self-care, which help build a more supportive inner environment. This can help reduce the shadow self's negative impact on our emotional well-being.

- Authenticity and Integration of suppressed aspects: Healing the inner child can help us accept and integrate suppressed aspects of ourselves, leading to a greater sense of authenticity and a more integrated self. This can help reduce the shadow self's negative impact on our self-image and sense of self.

By healing the inner child, we can gain a deeper understanding of our motivations, emotions, and behaviors and develop the ability to make positive changes. This can direct to a greater sense of self-awareness, emotional balance, and well-being and can help reduce the shadow self's negative impact on our thoughts, feelings, and behaviors.

In summary, healing the inner child can positively impact our shadow self. When you don't get the love, attention, praise, and other emotional support you need as a child, it can cause trauma that can last well into your adult life. But you can heal your inner child. By learning to take care of your inner child, you can reinforce these needs, be able to express emotions in healthy ways, and boost self-compassion and self-love.

As we work to heal the inner child, we may access repressed memories, challenge negative beliefs and thought patterns, process and release unresolved emotions, and accept and integrate suppressed aspects of ourselves. This can lead to greater self-awareness, emotional balance, and well-being. In the next chapter, you'll learn more about the shadow self.

Chapter 6:
The Shadow Self

W e can't start the healing process until we face our shadow self. Most of the time, people hide who they are. So, the question is: who or what is our shadow self?

Carl Jung's work in psychology and psychoanalysis is where the concept of "shadow self" comes from. The first book in which he laid out his thoughts on the unconscious mind and how he viewed the archetypes and their working was *The Psychology of the Unconscious*, published in 1912. After that, Carl Jung presented the idea of the shadow self in several of his books, but it's most notably discussed in his book *"Collected Works: The Archetypes and the Collective Unconscious"* published in 1959.

Jung thought that the human mind has both conscious and unconscious parts and that the unconscious part has both good and bad in it. He called the bad parts of the unconscious "the shadow," and he believed that this part of the self is made up of repressed feelings, desires, and impulses that often go against what we understand to be true and what we value. Jung said simply that the "shadow is whatever we don't want to know about ourselves." It has no fixed content; it includes whatever a particular culture considers unacceptable and must be repressed.

In childhood, we learn to consciously suppress whatever isn't acceptable to our social circle. We do that so that we can be accepted as an individual. For example, the anger you felt when scolded for throwing a tantrum may have been stored away, and you put on a more socially acceptable smile. Throughout your childhood, anger was viewed as undesirable. Anger, rage, jealousy, greed, and selfishness are all feelings that everyone experiences, but not everyone is comfortable expressing them. You may have suppressed these emotions or characteristics as a part of the shadow side of your personality. So, the shadow is this repressed and suppressed content in the unconscious mind.

Jung thought that the shadow is a natural and necessary part of the psyche and must be acknowledged and integrated for psychological wholeness. He believed the shadow could manifest itself in various ways, such as dreams and archetypes. He also thought that the shadow could show up as projections, in which people see their bad qualities in other people.

Jung's ideas about the shadow have made a big difference in psychology, and other theorists and practitioners have built on them. Today, the idea of the "shadow" is well-known in psychology, psychiatry, and psychotherapy. It's often used to understand and deal with emotional and behavioral problems. It's important to remember that the idea of the shadow self isn't unique to Jungian psychology. It has also been used in different spiritual and philosophical traditions, where it's often called the "dark side" or "negative self."

The shadow self can significantly impact an individual's behavior and well-being. Here are some ways that the shadow self can affect individuals:

- Repressed emotions: When the shadow self isn't acknowledged or accepted, it can lead to repressed emotions, which can manifest as physical or psychological symptoms.

- Negative patterns of behavior: Aspects of the shadow self can manifest as negative patterns of behavior such as anger, addiction, or procrastination.

- Difficulty forming healthy relationships: The shadow self can lead to difficulties forming healthy relationships, as repressed emotions and negative behavior patterns can create conflicts and misunderstandings. The shadow may cause you to be judgmental and point fingers at others' flaws. You could be tempted to play the victim by the shadow.

- Difficulty dealing with stress: When the shadow self isn't acknowledged or accepted, it can be harder to cope with stress and take responsibility for one's actions.

- Inability to express emotions: When the shadow self isn't acknowledged or accepted, it can be difficult to express emotions healthily, leading to isolation and dissatisfaction.

- Low self-esteem: The shadow self can lead to low self-esteem, as individuals may not be able to accept and integrate their negative traits and flaws into their overall sense of self.

- Difficulty dealing with change: When the shadow self isn't acknowledged or accepted, it can be difficult to adapt to new situations and make positive changes in one's life.

The question is, what happens when we force our shadow self deeper down the well? The further you bury it, the less you want to look at these aspects of who you are. The more severe your physical or mental problems, the greater the degree to which you'll be required to disconnect yourself from what is inside you.

A significant portion of individuals with personality disorders, most notably NPD, have a profoundly ingrained shadow that they stubbornly refuse to acknowledge. Because of this, the shadowy components will become more obvious, and the more you try to conceal them, the more they will become apparent. Therefore, repressing our shadows also has a spiritual and energetic component. The more we try to cover it up, the more the universe will conspire to place us in circumstances where we're compelled to face it. For instance, if you wish to act as if the death of a loved one doesn't touch you, the world will put you in circumstances that'll force you to go through the stages of grief.

"Shadow work" is the process of uncovering, accepting, and identifying your suppressed parts and understanding them. You consciously integrate your shadow rather than acting on it unconsciously. Shadow work aims to bring the hidden or repressed parts of the self, aka "shadow self," into conscious awareness to be understood, accepted, and integrated into the overall sense of self.

This process can help individuals better understand themselves and their motivations and identify patterns of behavior or thought that might be causing problems in their lives. There are many benefits of shadow work. It can, for example, lead to greater self-awareness and self-acceptance, improved relationships, and a sense of greater inner peace. It can help individuals overcome fears, phobias, and other emotional or behavioral issues.

Shadow work can also help individuals heal from past traumas or negative experiences by allowing them to confront and process the emotions associated with those experiences. Furthermore, it can help individuals understand and let go of patterns of behavior or thoughts that might hold them back.

Additionally, bringing the shadow self into conscious awareness can help in self-forgiveness and self-compassion. Understanding and accepting our negative traits and flaws can make extending that same understanding and compassion easier to others.

You can use shadow work to improve many different parts of your life. Here are a few examples of how shadow work can help you better care of yourself:

- Build up your confidence and sense of self-worth:

  Taking on yourself as the full version of yourself will give you greater confidence. You no longer have hidden doubts about parts of yourself that you might not like or even hate. This means that you can move toward your goals with more confidence. Shadow traits are often used as elements of our identity. However, if they're true weaknesses, you'll be better able to deal with them if you bring them to light so you can understand (and possibly better manage) them. The worst thing about our shadow is when we don't even know it's there.

- Find ways to be more creative:

  There's more to shadows than hiding what people think is wrong with you. It can also hide great things about you, like your creativity. When you accept your shadow, you can get in touch with your creative side. You don't have to hide your darker side. Instead, you can use all of the unique ways it shows itself.

- Get along better with other people:

  You can only love and accept others as much as you love and accept yourself when you can control what you think about others. You can see them for who they are. You no longer see them as mirrors of the parts of yourself you don't like. Because of this, you can get closer to them.

- Make it easy to exercise self-acceptance:

  When you push away your shadow, you can eliminate any unconscious self-hatred you might have. But you can only do this if you're self-aware and fully accept that part of yourself. Accepting your shadow means accepting and caring about every part of yourself. It won't come easily and naturally all the time. But when you start shadowing, you open the door to getting there.

- Helps to discover your hidden talents:

  The process of shadow work can help you discover inner strengths and resources you didn't know you had. Some people may worry that the darkness in their shadow is too much for them to handle. However, this golden shadow takes up most of the space most of the time. It just hadn't had a chance to grow before. Shadow work can entice this part of you to come out of hiding and let you do everything you're capable of.

- A sense of happiness and calm:

  After shadow work, people often say they feel more at peace than they ever imagined.

- Better sleep:

  For shadow work, getting into a deep, meditative state is similar to when we drift off to sleep. As you keep doing shadow work, it gets easier to get to sleep. Not only that, but people feel less anxious and depressed, so once they fall asleep, they stay asleep and wake up feeling relaxed and full of energy.

- Take care of your health in general:

  Trying to hide your shadow can cause a lot of trouble. You might not realize that these problems come from a part of you that you've been hiding until you're ready to face that shadow. By starting at the root, shadow work can help you take charge of your health journey. Instead of focusing on specific health problems, such as anxiety or bad relationships, shadow work focuses on what causes them.

- Able to show more kindness to other people:

  When you talk to other people, shadow work can help you stop projecting onto them. People's personality traits and habits are less likely to bother you. In turn, this can make you care more about other people. You no longer see the bad things about yourself in other people. Instead, you might see them as whole people who're probably fighting their battles inside.

- Make things clearer:

  Shadow work helps you see how your thoughts, feelings, and emotions make you act the way you do. When you have this information, you can be more clear and real about who you are.

- Lessen worry:

  Anxiety is caused by the ego mind, which is overridden by shadow work. With shadow work, your therapist will break the subconscious feedback loop, an internal control system that causes anxiety, and teaches you how to get rid of it for good.

- Depression went down:

  Shadow work helps people figure out the first thing that makes them depressed. During a shadow work session, we rewire that moment on many levels to free it from its hold. This causes a healing ripple effect. This is like pulling out a weed by its roots.

- Getting over PTSD:

  Shadow work rewrites your mind, body, emotional, and energetic system so that your traumas aren't stored the same way inside you. When this is done, the client's view of the event that caused their PTSD changes completely, which has a ripple effect of healing.

Some people might wonder if shadow work is dangerous. I think this question comes from the word "shadow," which is generally used to describe something dark, misunderstood, or maybe even related to dark magic. I'm going to tell you that shadow work isn't inherently evil and has nothing to do with using dark powers. The point of shadow work is to face your deepest fears, insecurities, and traumas that you have been trying to hide. It might not be "dangerous," but it can be a lot to deal with. The more you ignore and push down your shadow self, the darker and harder it will be to work through. You might even find out about traumas you didn't know you had. This can be exhausting, overwhelming, and even traumatic for people especially weak ones. On the other hand, doing your shadow work can lead to rewards that can completely change you.

You're changing how your subconscious mind works, which will change how you act. But it takes time, work, and discipline to do this. When you face your shadow self, you might change your habits and rethink your relationships, career, and even who you are. In the beginning, this can be a lot to handle, but it will help you get better. Even though it's not dangerous, you should be careful. If you feel too overwhelmed by emotions at any point, you should consult a mental health professional.

Shadow work can be a helpful way to improve yourself and grow as a person, but it can also be hard on your emotions and mind. It's essential to be aware of the risks and do shadow work carefully. One risk of shadow work is that it can make you feel too much guilt, shame, or hate for yourself. Keep in mind that the shadow self isn't inherently "bad." Instead, it's a normal and necessary part of the mind. Shadow work should be done with compassion and self-forgiveness, not judgment and punishment.

Shadow work can also make people more anxious and depressed. This can happen if a person isn't ready to face some parts of their shadow self or doesn't have the support or guidance they need. Before doing shadow work, you should think about how emotionally and mentally ready you are, and if you need to, you should get help from a professional.

In my opinion, not doing shadow work is the only thing that could be dangerous. People who don't know about their shadows repeat the same cycle of traumas and bad habits passed down from generation to generation. Some of them also have the same old bad feelings and thoughts.

So, it's important to approach shadow work in a healthy, balanced way and pay attention to your own emotional and mental state as you do it. Working with a therapist or counselor or joining a support group with others who do shadow work can be helpful. During shadow work, it's also important to take care of your body and mind by getting enough sleep, exercising, and taking care of yourself.

Various methods and techniques can be used for shadow work, and the best approach will depend on the individual's needs and preferences. Here are some common ways to start practicing shadow work:

- Journaling: Writing about your thoughts, feelings, and experiences can be a powerful tool for exploring the shadow self. You can use prompts or questions to focus your writing, such as "What are my fears?" or "What patterns of behavior or thought cause problems in my life?"

- Inner dialogue: Reflect on your thoughts and emotions and note negative self-talk or limiting beliefs. Challenge these thoughts with positive affirmations or by seeking evidence that contradicts them.

- Identify projections: Look out for situations where you find yourself getting easily irritated, annoyed, or frustrated with others, and try to identify the source of these feelings within yourself. This will help you understand the shadow material you're projecting on others.

- Active imagination: This technique involves using your imagination to enter into a dialogue with different parts of your personality, such as your inner child, inner critic, or shadow self. This can help you gain a deeper understanding of these aspects of yourself and to incorporate them into your overall sense of self.

- Embrace your shadow: Take some time to reflect on your shadow self, and try to understand and accept the darker parts of yourself. Embrace your shadows and try to see them as an integral part of who you are.

- Therapy: A therapist or counselor can provide guidance and support as you explore your shadow self. They can help you identify patterns of behavior or thoughts that might be causing problems in your life and understand the underlying emotions and beliefs that drive them.

- Meditation: Meditation can help you quiet the mind and become more aware of your thoughts, feelings, and sensations. This can be a powerful tool for exploring the shadow self and gaining insight into your motivations and behavior patterns.

- Dream analysis: Dreams can provide a window into the unconscious mind and reveal aspects of the shadow self. Keeping a dream journal and reflecting on your dreams' symbolism and meaning can be helpful.

- Reflective practices: Reflecting on your own experiences, behaviors, and emotions can also be a powerful tool for exploring the shadow self. It can be helpful to ask yourself questions like "Why did I react that way?" or "What do I believe about myself?"

Remember that shadow work is an ongoing process, and it's likely that new aspects of the shadow will continue to emerge as you grow and evolve. It's a lifelong journey of self-discovery and self-improvement.

Shadow work can be a sensitive and personal journey, and it's important to work at your own pace and be mindful of your own emotional and psychological state throughout the process. It can be helpful to seek professional help and care for yourself physically and emotionally during the shadow work process by getting enough sleep, exercising, and self-care.

Here are some signs that your shadow work practice may be working:

- Increased self-awareness: You may find that you have a better understanding of your thoughts, feelings, and behaviors, as well as the motivations behind them.

- Improved relationships: Shadow work can help you to understand and let go of patterns of behavior or thoughts that might be causing problems in your relationships. Thus, you may find that your relationships improve.

- Greater sense of inner peace: Shadow work can help you understand and accept your darker aspects, leading to a superior sense of inner peace and self-acceptance.

- Overcoming fears and phobias: As you explore your shadow self, you may find that you can better understand and overcome fears and phobias that are holding you back.

- Increased ability to express emotions: As you gain a deeper understanding of your own emotions, you may find that you can better healthily express them.

- Decrease in negative self-talk or limiting beliefs: As you work through your shadow self, you may have less negative self-talk or limiting beliefs.

- Greater sense of self-compassion and self-forgiveness: Shadow work can help you understand and accept the darker parts of yourself, leading to greater self-compassion and self-forgiveness.

It's important to remember that progress may not always be linear, and sometimes you may experience setbacks or moments of feeling stuck. That's normal and part of the process. It's crucial to be kind and compassionate with yourself and seek professional help if needed.

As discussed in this chapter, the shadow self refers to the parts of the psyche that are hidden or repressed, often including negative traits, fears, and repressed emotions. In individuals with NPD, the shadow self can include feelings of inadequacy and vulnerability, which they may try to conceal through grandiose behavior and an inflated sense of self-importance.

In a narcissistic individual, the shadow self is often associated with a fear of being seen as weak or inferior, and they may use various defense mechanisms, such as denial, projection, and blame-shifting, to avoid confronting and accepting this aspect of themselves. As a result, they may have trouble forming genuine relationships and struggle with feelings of emptiness or dissatisfaction. In contrast, in an emotionally stable individual, the shadow self is also present, but they can recognize, acknowledge and accept it as a natural part of themselves. They may use different coping mechanisms to deal with it, such as self-reflection and self-compassion, to integrate it into their overall sense of self. They may also have healthy relationships and can express their feelings and emotions healthily. In the next chapter, we will discuss more about the shadow self of narcissistic people.

Chapter 7:
The Shadow Self and Narcissism

I n the previous chapter, we went over the idea of one's shadow self and the method of engaging in shadow work. In this chapter, we'll explore how these theories can be applied to people who display narcissistic traits.

I hope you can learn more about narcissism by distinguishing between a narcissistic public persona and a private self. We all have a personality we reveal when we're with others, whether with their family, friends, work, or public. But we also have a "shadow self," which is everything deep inside our personality. It's a complete and complicated picture of who we are. It has many different sides. We all have strengths deep inside. We also bring our limitations to the table. At different times, we can feel afraid and unsure of ourselves. There are times when different things bother us. Sometimes we have trouble with shame or guilt or don't know what to do. We've all made mistakes and learned from them, and we've all done some things well, but we also have many flaws that make us who we are.

Narcissism is a personality disorder characterized by excessive self-importance, a lack of compassion, and a need for admiration and validation. The development of the shadow self in narcissists is affected by the defense mechanisms they use to protect their inflated sense of self-worth and maintain their self-image.

One of the main defense mechanisms used by narcissists is repression, where they push unwanted thoughts, feelings, and memories into the unconscious mind. This includes any traits or aspects of themselves that they perceive as negative or unimportant, such as vulnerability, insecurity, and empathy. These repressed aspects of the self become part of the shadow self, the unconscious aspect of the personality that contains the repressed and denied aspects of the self.

Another defense mechanism narcissists use is denial, where they refuse to acknowledge or accept certain aspects of themselves or reality. This includes traits or behaviors that threaten their self-image or challenge their sense of superiority, such as mistakes, flaws, or criticism. The denial of these aspects of the self also contributes to forming the shadow self. Therefore, the narcissist's shadow self is formed by the repressed and denied aspects of the self that don't align with their inflated sense of self-worth and idealized self-image. This shadow self can be highly destructive to the narcissist and those around them, as it can manifest in harmful behaviors and attitudes.

Narcissists need to keep a tight grip on their appearance. They want to be in charge of every situation and be the ones to dictate the terms of any relationship. They want to be given special treatment and care so much about how people see them in public that they've pushed down their private selves to the point where they act as if they don't even exist. Narcissists tend to put much effort into maintaining their public selves. They often strive to present a perfect image to the world that is polished and in control. They're particularly sensitive to perceived flaws or weaknesses in their public selves and will go to great lengths to hide or deny them. They have a strong need for admiration and validation, and they use their public selves to gain this attention and approval from others.

The traits of the shadow self in narcissists can vary depending on the individual, but some common ones include:

- Vulnerability: The narcissist's shadow self may contain repressed feelings of vulnerability and insecurity, which they may not be able to acknowledge or accept. This can make them feel weak or exposed, and they may avoid showing vulnerability or seeking help.

- Empathy: Narcissists may lack the ability to empathize with others, as they may have repressed their ability to appreciate and relate to the feelings of others. They may be seen as callous, indifferent, or manipulative in their relationships with others.

- Shame: Narcissists may have a strong sense of shame associated with their shadow self, as they may perceive their flaws, mistakes, and negative traits as a reflection of their inherent worthlessness. They may also be highly sensitive to criticism or rejection and react with anger or defensiveness.

- Dependence: Narcissists may depend on external validation and admiration, as they may have repressed self-doubt and insecurity. They may constantly need attention and praise and be highly affected by negative feedback or rejection.

- Manipulation: Narcissists may engage in manipulative behaviors, as they may repress their own needs and desires and instead focus on getting what they want from others. They may use charm, flattery, or deceit to control or exploit others.

Narcissists tend to have a strong fear and aversion to their shadow selves. They're highly resistant to self-reflection and tend to avoid introspection that might bring their hidden aspects to light. They're not willing to acknowledge the existence of their shadow selves, let alone work on integrating them into their conscious selves. They prefer to focus on maintaining their public selves and the image they present to the world rather than facing the uncomfortable truths about themselves that lie within their shadow selves.

Additionally, narcissists tend to see themselves as perfect, so they don't find any need for personal growth or self-improvement. This is why narcissists rarely engage in shadow work, and when they do, it's usually on a superficial level to fix a specific behavior or trait that's causing them problems in their personal or professional life.

Ultimately, their public character is a form of enslavement for them. The narcissist's persona will become their master as soon as they commit to a particular identity and refuse to look at what's lurking in the shadows of their character. It appears they struggle to control an addiction when they say, "No, I have to be the best; I have to be the strongest." Usually, increasing amounts of an addictive substance or behavior are necessary to achieve the desired effect. Over and over again, they'll return to the same power dynamics until they're no longer free. Their issues, pressures, and tensions drive them crazy, and because they can't break free of the cage they've created for themselves, they put on this fake persona. Finally, the narcissist's public persona would crumble to pieces.

Grandiose and vulnerable narcissism are two distinct subtypes of NPD. A sense of self-importance characterizes grandiose narcissism, a need for appreciation, and a lack of empathy. Feelings of insecurity and a need for validation characterize vulnerable narcissism.

So, is it likely for a narcissist to present with both traits? Yes, an individual can exhibit traits of grandiose and vulnerable narcissism, as technically, they're not mutually exclusive and can coexist within the same person. The shadow self can explain this phenomenon as the fragile, insecure aspects of the self that a grandiose narcissist represses or denies. This individual may present a facade of confidence and self-importance to the world, but deep down, they may feel intensely insecure and need validation.

The 2011 study by Brad J. Bushman et al., *Grandiose and Vulnerable Narcissism: A Nomological Network Analysis,* looked at the relationship between grandiose and vulnerable narcissism by analyzing data from a group of undergraduate students. The study found that the two types of narcissism are different but related. Grandiose narcissism is more closely linked to extraversion, while vulnerable narcissism is more closely linked to neuroticism. The study also found that grandiose and vulnerable narcissism have similar links to other personality traits and disorders like aggression, impulsivity, and depression.

The second article, *Grandiose and Vulnerable Narcissism: A Review of the Literature* also by Brad J. Bushman et al. (2016), is a review article that gives a comprehensive overview of the existing literature on the topic. This article also concluded that grandiose and vulnerable narcissism are two types of NPD that are related but have different traits. For example, grandiose narcissism is marked by a sense of self-importance, a need for appreciation, and a lack of empathy. On the other hand, someone with vulnerable narcissism feels insecure and needs to be validated. The article also found that both types of narcissism are linked to similar outcomes, such as aggression, impulsivity, and depression.

Both articles say that the fact that grandiose and vulnerable narcissism exists simultaneously can be explained by the fact that the two types of narcissism are different but related and that a person can have traits of both types.

Someone narcissistic can change and evolve like other people. The problem is that they won't gain the power and strength they need to develop moral responsibility and healthier ways to cope as long as they don't reflect on themselves, distort reality, project negatives, self-aggrandize, play the victim, and disconnect emotionally from others. It starts as a childhood defense against feelings of unlovability but becomes a self-fulfilling trap that prevents trust and connection.

These behaviors can make it difficult for narcissists to maintain healthy relationships, as their partners may feel neglected, manipulated, or disrespected. But not every narcissist behaves similarly, and their behavior can change depending on different situations and individuals.

Narcissists' refusal to self-reflect allows them to repress their shame and avoid seeing how their grandiosity affects others. This prevents them from developing self-awareness and learning from their mistakes. They also hold facts at a distance and substitute lies and distortions that conform to their inflated self-beliefs. Narcissistic people are emotionally dysregulated, self-serving, and profoundly traumatizing to others. Playing the victim is also a strategy to get others' attention, sympathy, and care. Standing far from their humanity is meant to buffer them from vulnerability but keeps them fear-driven, rigid, and isolated.

The potential for the shadow self to cause harm to the narcissist is also significant. The repressed and denied aspects of the self that make up the shadow self can manifest in harmful behaviors and attitudes that can negatively impact narcissists. Some ways that the shadow self can cause harm to the narcissist include:

- Difficulty forming genuine connections: Narcissists may find it hard to form genuine connections with others, which can lead to feelings of solitude and isolation.

- Inability to handle criticism: Narcissists may be highly sensitive to criticism or rejection, leading to feelings of shame, inadequacy, and low self-esteem.

- Dependence on external validation: Narcissists may have a sense of dependence on external validation and admiration, making them vulnerable to manipulation and exploitation by others.

- Inability to take responsibility: Narcissists may have difficulty taking responsibility for their actions, making it difficult for them to make amends or change negative behaviors.

- Inability to cope with reality: Narcissists may have a distorted perception of reality due to the repression and denial of certain aspects of self and reality, leading to difficulties in decision-making, problem-solving, and adapting to change.

- Difficulty in accepting change: Narcissists may find it hard to accept change, as it may threaten their idealized self-image and sense of self-worth.

Facing and accepting the shadow self is an important step in healing from narcissism, as it allows the individual to integrate the repressed and denied aspects of the self and to develop a more authentic and healthy sense of self.

One of the main reasons why facing and accepting the shadow self is important is because repressing and denying certain aspects of the self can lead to harmful behaviors and attitudes. By facing and accepting the shadow self, the individual can take responsibility for their actions, make amends, and change negative behaviors. This can improve their relationships and overall well-being.

Facing and accepting the shadow self can also help alleviate feelings of shame, inadequacy, and low self-esteem that may have been caused by repressing and denying certain aspects of the self. It allows the individual to acknowledge and accept their flaws, mistakes, and negative traits and to develop a more realistic and balanced sense of self-worth.

Furthermore, facing and accepting the shadow self can help improve the individual's ability to empathize, connect with others, and form healthy relationships. It allows them to understand, relate to and care about the feelings of others, which can lead to more satisfying and meaningful relationships.

In short, facing and accepting the shadow self is important in healing from narcissism. It allows the individual to integrate the repressed and denied aspects of the self, take responsibility for their actions, alleviate feelings of shame and low self-esteem, and improve relationships and overall well-being.

Narcissists are so preoccupied with their outside appearance that they can't go inward and discover what is lurking in the shadows of their minds. Because of this, all of the confusion, tension, and difficulties that are lurking in the background become dominant on a subconscious level, and as a result, they don't continue to escalate.

They don't gain any knowledge, so it's important to emphasize that the first step toward development and wellness is being truthful about what's happening, which narcissists find very difficult to do, honestly.

Now, as you compare your public persona to what's going on within your "shadow self," I hope you'll be able to recognize areas in which you need to make some adjustments, so you can acquire the ability to work toward bringing these two aspects as close to one another as possible. You can't possibly give everyone an accurate picture of who you are on the inside, however, I do hope that you can spend time with some significant others so that your shadow self will not be as powerful in the future as it is right now. Being truthful, genuine, and consistent in your life is one way to differentiate yourself from your narcissistic self.

I hope reading this book will help you learn more about yourself and your life. Several techniques can be used to help heal and integrate the shadow self. Some of these techniques include:

- Therapy: Therapy can be an effective way to help heal and integrate the shadow self. A therapist can help the individual understand the underlying causes of their narcissism and identify and process the repressed and denied aspects of the self. Therapy can also help individuals to develop healthier coping mechanisms, improve their ability to empathize, and form healthier relationships.

- Self-reflection: Self-reflection is important in healing and integrating the shadow self. This can include journaling, meditating, or self-inquiry exercises. Self-reflection can help the individual identify and process repressed thoughts, feelings, and memories.

- Mindfulness: Mindfulness practices can help the individual become more conscious and mindful of their thoughts, feelings, and behaviors, which can help them identify repressed and denied aspects of the self. Mindfulness practices can also help the individual develop a more authentic and healthy sense of self.

- Acceptance: Acceptance is an important step in healing and integrating the shadow self. This includes accepting the repressed and denied aspects of the self, accepting the past and learning from it, and accepting the present moment. Determine the meaning of your emotions, attitudes, reactions, and behaviors with complete accuracy. Simply be upfront and honest about what's happening inside you and remember that it's all right to say things like, "I struggle just like the rest of you. I feel confused. I feel inadequate and afraid. The rejections I've received have left marks on me. I can't just point the finger at others for all my difficulties. At some point, it's incumbent upon me to accept responsibility for the person I am. I feel embarrassed."

- Empathy: Developing empathy can help the individual connect with others and understand and relate to the feelings of others, which can help integrate the shadow self.

- Self-compassion: Self-compassion can help the individual have a more realistic and balanced sense of self-worth, which can help integrate the shadow self.

Therapy can play an important role in healing from narcissism. A therapist can help the individual to understand the underlying causes of their narcissism and identify and process the repressed and denied aspects of the self that make up the shadow self.

Cognitive Behavioral Therapy can be an effective therapy for narcissism. It can help individuals identify and change negative thoughts, beliefs, and behaviors that contribute to narcissism. This can help the individual develop a more authentic and healthy sense of self and to improve their relationships and overall well-being.

Another effective form of therapy is psychoanalytic therapy, which can help the person understand the unconscious reasons behind their narcissism and identify and process repressed thoughts, feelings, and memories. This can help the individual develop insight, self-awareness, and self-compassion, which can aid in their healing process.

In addition, Family Systems therapy can address the impact of narcissism on the family and relationships and improve communication and understanding among family members.

In this chapter, we went over the concept of the "shadow self" in narcissism and how it's formed through the defense mechanisms of repression and denial. We've explored the characteristics of the shadow self in narcissists, the impact it can have on their relationships, and the potential for it to cause harm to both the narcissist and others. We've also highlighted the importance of facing and accepting the shadow self as a crucial step in healing from narcissism.

In the upcoming chapters, we will delve deeper into healing from narcissism and discuss various techniques and strategies for improving the shadow self. We will explore different forms of therapy, such as Cognitive Behavioral Therapy and psychoanalytic therapy, that can aid in the healing process. Additionally, we will discuss the importance of self-reflection, mindfulness, acceptance, empathy, and self-compassion as tools for integrating the shadow self. We will also examine the impact of narcissism on family and relationships and ways to improve communication and understanding among family members. It's important to remember that healing from narcissism is a lifelong process that requires commitment, patience, and self-compassion. By improving our shadow self, we can develop a more authentic and healthy sense of self and improve our relationships and overall well-being.

Chapter 8:
Can a Narcissist Change?

I n the previous chapters, we explored NPD in detail and what causes narcissism in a person, and how these personality traits affect their lives, relationships, and careers. An important point arises: now you know that you have NPD, and you know what these characteristics are, and how they have affected your whole life. Now, what should you do? What could be the next step, what's the chance that NPD can be treated, and can you ever have an emotionally stable and healthy life with stable affections, feelings, and emotions?

Yes, a narcissist can change, but that requires a significant amount of effort and self-reflection on their part, as well as support and understanding from those around them. It isn't an easy process, and it may take a long time for a person with narcissistic traits to understand and address their behavior fully. However, with the right approach and resources, change is possible.

The problem with narcissists has never been that they can't change. It's that most narcissists don't want to change. To change a bad habit, a person must first admit that it's bad.

Most of the time, they don't want to (or can't) do that. However, the narcissist can be pushed to. For a narcissist to change, they have to be able to realize that their actions are what is making them feel bad. They must dislike how the behavior makes them feel so much that they don't want to feel that way anymore. They need to understand that the way they act is a choice. Even when upset, they should be able to see when a choice is being made and change it.

Even though it seems strange, people with NPD tend to have a very low sense of self, so they must constantly tell others they're important and valuable and get confirmation from them. So, if a person with NPD is self-aware enough to realize that they feel empty inside or don't think they're worth much, that's a pretty good start. Also, if they're actively looking for help and agreeing to get it on their own, that could signify that they're willing to change.

Another big part of the problem is that many of the narcissist's actions are deeply ingrained habits and patterns. They permitted themselves to act the way they did years ago, and people around them helped them keep that permission. they're like children: if a behavior is rewarded, it'll be done again. When narcissists throw fits or get violent, they've likely been like that their whole lives. They do it when they're upset. They've been doing this for so long that they don't even think about it anymore, and they keep doing it because it works for them. Since this behavior has been reinforced and repeated for so long, they may no longer feel like they have a choice. They might say it "just happens," and they can't do anything about it. There's nothing wrong with them, but they don't think before acting, so they don't control what they do.

If the narcissist could be forced to think before they act, their choice not to follow bad habits is usually based on the consequences they have considered. It's possible to break the pattern if they are forced to think before acting. Then, maybe they switch to a new pattern and Don't revert to their old behavior. It's a unique situation, but it shows that narcissists can change their behavior if confronted with severe enough internal and external consequences.

The negative external consequences may have been the vehicle for behavior modification, but the negative internal consequences are the ones that change behavior. The change would not have been permanent if it was solely based on external consequences. This is true for most behavior modifications and most motivations for change. If people don't feel it, it won't last. In contrast, due to their disorder, narcissists find it more difficult to understand that their behavior is problematic. When a narcissist feels justified in their behavior, it's very difficult to realize that something is wrong or should change. It can't be wrong when there's a reason for it, can it?

There's no doubt that narcissists understand right from wrong. They believe they didn't do anything wrong because they have "reasons" which are always their feelings. People are responsible for their feelings and their reactions to them. Narcissists believe they merely react to things around them rather than control them. Behavior can't be changed as long as they consider this as truth.

They must understand that this behavior is a choice they're exercising and they must be able to recognize when the choice is being considered and choose a different one - even when they're upset.

The key to overcoming narcissistic tendencies is incremental progress. Health and wellness expert Caleb Backe recaps what the uphill journey will entail: "One of the key ways that narcissists can identify their need to change is through meaningful consequences. There needs to be motivation for them and their own needs that would benefit them if they become less narcissistic. Whether this is the possibility of losing a loved one or the threat of losing their job, there needs to be a trigger for them to see that they need to alter their ways." The "bottom-out" process inspires the idea of maintaining motivation. Acquiring and maintaining the motivation for change comes from understanding what's at stake if they don't change and what's to gain if they do. Setting boundaries and being more mindful are all ways to enhance their understanding of why this change is so important and necessary.

As we know, there are different kinds of narcissism, and each behaves differently. Covert narcissists, for example, may seem weaker and more insecure than they are. Their actions might be more passive-aggressive and clever, which can be hard for people who care about them to understand. A communal narcissist is more likely to care about being important in society. They think it's important to have a strong mission or purpose, and they may act like martyrs. Lastly, a malignant narcissist is a lot like a sociopath. Narcissistic sociopaths often enjoy hurting others to meet their needs and may have the hardest time changing their behavior.

Change has to come from within for a person with NPD, just like it does for anyone else. If someone with NPD went to therapy "for a relationship," they probably wouldn't change in the long run because they wouldn't be invested in the process for any reason other than to make the other person happy. For real change to happen, they have to want to be different and be willing to put in the work. This requires them to see how weak they are and how they contribute to the toxic nature of the relationship. This is the hardest part for people with NPD.

So, how to tell if someone is ready to change? Several indicators suggest that someone is open to analyzing their behavior and exploring alternatives. These signs include:

- Respecting others' feelings:

  Narcissism is often associated with a lack of empathy. However, research suggests that empathy isn't always absent among people with narcissistic tendencies. When motivated, narcissists can develop greater empathy, by adopting the perspective of someone similar in particular, when it comes to their children or others who value and idealize them. When individuals show concern for certain people, they may be ready for further therapy changes.

- Attention to their behavior:

    People who wonder why they behave in certain ways may be open to exploring their behavior in therapy. The interest might develop when someone points out their narcissistic tendencies or after reading articles or books about narcissism. Despite their traits, narcissistic people can live fairly stable and healthy lives. An intelligent and ambitious person may be interested not only in their behavior but also in the behavior of others. Seeing other people as equals rather than inferiors can result from this.

- Self-reflection:

    People with narcissism may have difficulty reflecting on themselves because it damages their protective shell. Narcissism is characterized by the inability to see that all people have positive and negative characteristics (called whole object relations). Rather, most narcissistic individuals see others, including themselves, as either entirely good (perfect) or entirely bad (worthless). They might respond by lashing out or spiraling into shame and self-hatred if their assumption of perfection is challenged. It may be possible to explore negative behaviors in more depth for those who can examine and reflect on them without devaluing the critic or themselves.

There are several difficulties that individuals with NPD may face when trying to change their behavior. Some of these include:

- Difficulty accepting responsibility: Narcissists often have difficulty accepting that their behavior is problematic and may blame others for their problems. This can make it hard for them to take responsibility for their actions and make positive changes.

- Lack of self-awareness: Narcissists may have a limited understanding of their behavior and its impact on others. This can make it challenging for them to recognize the need for change and to understand what changes are necessary.

- Inability to empathize: Narcissists often lack empathy and may have a hard time understanding the perspectives and feelings of others. This can make it tough for them to develop the empathy and understanding necessary for positive change.

- Difficulty regulating emotions: Narcissists may have difficulty managing and controlling their emotions, making it difficult for them to make positive changes.

- Resistance to change: Narcissists may resist change, as they may see themselves as perfect and may not understand why they need to change.

- Difficulty in trusting others: Narcissists may have difficulty trusting others, making it difficult for them to form healthy relationships and accept help and support.

- Difficulty in accepting criticism: Narcissists may have difficulty accepting criticism, which can make it difficult for them to learn from their mistakes and make positive changes.

- Difficulty in admitting vulnerability: Narcissists may have difficulty admitting vulnerability, making it difficult for them to open up and be honest with themselves and others.

- Fear of rejection and abandonment: Narcissists may fear rejection and abandonment, making it difficult for them to take risks necessary for positive change.

- Difficulty in maintaining progress: Even when progress is made, it's not easy to maintain progress without consistent effort and support.

Again, I want to remind you that change is a difficult process, and it may take months or even years of therapy and personal work for the individual to make significant progress, but with the right approach and support, change is possible.

The narcissist should do a few things as part of the change process. It would be best if you stopped acting like you know everything to make the right changes. First, you need to start with a humble attitude and say, "I know; it's not all about me," or "You're on the learning curve when you start making changes." Say to yourself, "I want to learn because I don't know a lot," or "I like to hear what other people have to say," or "I'm excited about that." So, you should be willing to listen to what other people have to say if you want to change.

Secondly, get together with people you know, trust, and think will tell you the truth. Ask them, "What have you noticed about me that I need to pay special attention to?" And if they say some negative things about you, tell them "I appreciate you're saying that. Do you have some examples of what you mean?" Let other people tell you what they think or give you advice.

The third step in your change or growth process is to be clear about what you think needs to be fixed in yourself. Let's not forget something very important. People do a lot of nice, good, and admirable things. But each of us has problems, and we've done things that didn't go as planned, or we've made mistakes or miscalculated. Sometimes we wish we could take back actions or situations we landed in and mistakes we regret. Each of us is broken differently. And if you want to be someone who says, "I need to change," name your brokenness and talk about what you see on the inside, like your bad temper, judgmental nature, stubbornness, or defensiveness. Be very specific when you tell yourself what needs to change on the inside. Instead of saying, "I want to change," hold yourself accountable to people you trust.

The fourth point is that you can't just think about it and be done with it. Choose people who care about you, love you, and want to walk with you. This could be a close friend, a counselor, a support group, a relative, or anyone else you trust. Tell them what you're doing and be responsible for it. It can be helpful to feel like you and the people around you are all in this together and want to go in the same direction. Make sure that accountability is part of how you make changes.

Step five of the process of changing is to be ready to right the wrongs you've done. As you change and tell people, "I want to be a different person," you should be willing to make it up to them. Some people could be hurt by the things you've done in the past. Be willing to talk to those people about it. "I'm sorry for what I've said or done that has hurt you. I'm thinking about what I could do to make things better." Please be patient, and be ready to possibly get rejected. Try again. Don't just say you want to be a better person; show it by being good and kind, helping others, correcting your mistakes, and other similar things.

Lastly, number six is learning as much as possible about healthy living. There are a lot of good books, videos, seminars, and workshops you can go to, but make sure you're the kind of person who says, "I want to learn," not just, "I want to do better." And that's pretty much all there is to it. Make sure to learn how to live a healthy life and how to be a good person and get along with others.

You should know that this isn't something that'll happen overnight. It takes time. I hope you can decide on the most important things you want to be known for. I just wrote down a few things that are part of the change process. So, to stop being narcissistic, you should work on being good; not just pose as a good person in front of others. Keep your emotions in check. Stop yourself when you want to yell, be critical, or act impatient. Slow down and be patient to find out what's happening in other people's lives. Promise to tell the truth. Be true to yourself. Tell the truth about some of your successes and some of your failures. This is a healthy trait, and it points to another healthy trait: listening to what other people say. If somebody says something you don't agree with, think to yourself, "I wonder what's going on behind the scenes in their lives. Why do they think that way?" Think of yourself as a part of a community. Be polite and realize that what you think, say, and do will affect other people, and make sure you act in a way that helps people and not just your own needs. Make a promise to have a gentle spirit instead of being harsh, dominant, or forceful.

If you're wondering, "Can I change?" It's possible that the higher you're on that narcissism scale, the harder it will be. But don't give up and push yourself to try harder. Now could be a good time for you to say, "It's time for me to change." I hope that is something you're at least willing to consider.

In this chapter, we went over the importance of trying to stop being narcissists and avoiding the need to be the center of attention. This includes acknowledging your need for validation and attention and learning to empathize with others and focus on their needs. By making this effort, individuals with NPD can break the cycle of self-centered behavior and develop healthier relationships.

In the next chapter, we will delve further into this topic and discuss specific strategies and techniques for stopping the need to be the center of attention and start focusing on the needs and feelings of others.

Chapter 9:
How to Stop Being the Center of Attention

N arcissists have an attention-seeking attitude because they have an excessive need for admiration and validation. There's an inflated sense of self-importance among them, and they believe they're superior to others. They often have a grandiose sense of self, meaning they overestimate their abilities and accomplishments. A deep-seated insecurity or fear of rejection and abandonment may drive this attention-seeking behavior. Narcissists may also use attention-seeking behavior to manipulate and control others. It can be a way for them to assert dominance over those around them and feel in control.

Attention-seeking attitude is very common in children. It's easy to misinterpret children's attention-seeking behavior. Children seeking attention may ask for assistance doing something they can and have demonstrated before. Another example would be a child interrupting their parent on the phone while they know they're on the phone. You can work on resolving these behaviors in children and teach them better coping skills. In addition, you can give them structure with expectations of when their parents will devote their full attention to them.

In adults, attention-seeking behaviors can be conscious or unconscious attempts to gain affirmation or admiration by becoming the center of attention. To gain attention, a person can say or do something to get others' attention.

There's a difference between getting attention and seeking attention. As a result of healthy attention, we feel validated, understood, and loved. In contrast, attention-seeking behaviors make others uncomfortable by making them feel obligated to give attention rather than wanting to do so with no prompting.

Potential causes of attention-seeking behavior in adults include:

- Low self-esteem
- Loneliness
- Anxiety
- Jealousy
- Fixation on drama
- Unresolved trauma

Several psychiatric disorders can involve attention-seeking behavior and they are:

- Histrionic Personality Disorder (HPD)
- Narcissistic Personality Disorder (NPD)
- Borderline Personality Disorder (BPD)
- Antisocial Personality Disorder (ASPD)
- Attention-Deficit Hyperactivity Disorder (ADHD)

Among those disorders, NPD is characterized by an excessive desire for attention and admiration.

Some common signs of attention-seeking behavior include:

- Constantly seeking validation or reassurance from others
- Exaggerating or fabricating stories for attention
- Being excessively dramatic or emotional in situations
- Constantly interrupting or dominating conversations
- Constantly posting about oneself on social media
- Being overly concerned with one's appearance or image
- Needing to be the center of attention in social situations.

When you're a narcissist, if you're addicted to social media, you might just be addicted to the attention it gives you. You might even have withdrawals if you're not on it for an hour or more. If you feel depressed or bad about yourself when you don't get "enough" likes on a photo, you have a problem. If you're an attention seeker, you'll take it personally when others offend you. You want people's lives to revolve around you and nobody else. You're fishing for those likes and comments that say how good you're looking - which, you must admit, is the main reason you went to the gym. You might be an attention seeker if you document every second of your life on social media.

When you care so much about your image and reputation, you pretend to be nice to anyone and everyone you come across. You want to portray the perfect impression, so most people like you desperately. As an attention seeker, you lead people on and play with their feelings to seek validation. You tell everyone how you went on that amazing beach vacation or how you only charter flights or use a private jet. You constantly seek attention from others by flirting outrageously, smiling at them, or batting your lashes from afar.

Some other examples of attention-seeking behavior in real life include:

- A student who constantly interrupts the teacher or calls out answers in class to be recognized

- An employee who constantly talks about their accomplishments to their coworkers to be praised

- A person who exaggerates the details of their personal life or experiences to gain sympathy or admiration

- A person who's always looking for drama and making everything about them

- A person who always needs to be the center of attention in social gatherings

- A person who's always seeking validation and praise from others

Attention-seeking behavior is quite often indicative of deep-seated insecurities.

Why do people find it annoying when someone wants to be the center of attention? Normal conversation and life sometimes focus on Person A, Person B, Person C, and so on. The attention, focus, and interest of any informal group will shift. That makes sense. It doesn't mean you don't like the person who's not talking anymore. And emotionally stable people aren't only fine with that, but they like it because it gives them a chance to hear different points of view, learn from others, and keep the conversation moving fairly.

Narcissistic people are often accused of taking over conversations. Once the narcissist joins the conversation, people may start to get used to them and realize that the conversation is more about the narcissist talking and everyone else listening. So, people start to see conversations with narcissists more as performances than as a back-and-forth exchange. Now, let's face it: other people don't like this. They may put up with it, but they don't like it. They don't like it when other people talk over them. Don't be the person who makes them roll their eyes. If you're narcissistic and think people are just putting up with you, it can make you feel bad that they don't want to listen to you. People don't like it when others always want to be the center of attention. They might be amused for a minute, but then they'll be too tired to care.

I've already said that not all narcissists are aware of or want this attention. When they're the center of attention, vulnerable narcissists, sometimes called "covert narcissists," show a lot of social anxiety. So, they might not want to be the center of attention, but they disdain the conversations around them because they think they know more or are wasting their time with the people around them. So that sounds a little bit different. But it takes away from the experience of the person who's the center of attention at that moment.

What are you supposed to do?

- You need to learn how to listen. Even if you don't want to, you should make yourself listen to someone without talking over them. Learning this skill, which not many people have, can take you a long way.

- Ask people questions and pay attention to what they say. Narcissistic people can sometimes be interested, especially when they're love-bombing or trying to win someone over at the beginning of a relationship. Ask them a question about their experience to get them to keep talking about it. It won't be easy for you to do this, but you might end up learning something over time.

- Don't interrupt other people. Some people in certain cultures interrupt more than others when people are talking. But even with that in mind, most of us don't like it. Listen for the break. Depending on the situation, that could mean waiting for a natural pause, raising your hand, or letting someone finish what they were saying. Interrupting is a telltale sign of a narcissist's need to be the center of attention. It can also be a sign of entitlement, dominance, or just a lack of social awareness. If you interrupt a person, say, "I'm so sorry, I cut you off."

- Deal with the discomfort of not being the center of attention. If you have NPD, your biggest challenge will be the discomfort of becoming invisible. Most of a narcissist's automatic behaviors, like reacting, getting angry, interrupting, and wanting to be the center of attention, are meant to protect the ego. So, if you don't do them, your ego is just out there getting hurt. And that's all right. As children, it seemed like the end of the world when we didn't get what we wanted. But as adults, we live with ego injuries all the time, and we're fine. We roll with it. Take a deep breath and silently reassure the ego that everything will be fine. Think of not being the center of attention as a chance to relax and learn from other people. It's always tiring to want to be the center of attention.

- Make a list of the issues you're insecure about and how you act out to overcompensate for these supposed shortcomings. Ask yourself whether the attention you get from acting out is doing anything to make you feel more secure or confident. Consider what motivates you to seek attention and how it makes you feel. Observe the consequences afterward. Attention seekers often have control issues. There's no way you can get other people to do what you want. Expecting too much from others will lead to disappointment. You'll be surprised at how much better things turn out when you focus on controlling the only thing you can control, yourself.

- A person who's considered an attention seeker is likely to behave in an inauthentic manner. Painting, writing, and crafting are all great ways of expressing yourself authentically. It's okay to use social media constructively, but if you're using it to get attention, you should reconsider before you post. Volunteering your time to help others is a great way to show how much you care about

95

them. Don't compare yourself to others, as this can make you feel inadequate.

- See what you can learn from your past mistakes and forgive yourself. Don't worry about what people think; act in a way that feels genuine to you. You can accept yourself more easily if you develop personal affirmations. Commit to changing or eliminating your attention-seeking behavior. Every day or every week, write down your goals, such as "I'll meditate for five minutes."

- Those who seek attention tend to spend time with others. Establish a daily or weekly goal for how much time you'll spend alone. The root cause of your attention-seeking can be addressed by identifying your desire. If you confront these issues, you can overcome your attention-seeking tendencies.

- Attention-seeking behavior is often associated with addictive behavior and personality types. If you're aware of any other addictions or compulsive behaviors in yourself, join a support group. Seek a therapist for individual sessions or see if they have group therapy.

Here are a few other strategies that may help address attention-seeking behavior:

- Practice self-reflection: try to identify why you need to seek attention and validation from others. Are you looking to fill a void or mask insecurities? Understanding the underlying causes of your behavior can help you address them more effectively.

- Learn to set boundaries: It's important to understand that you can't always be the center of attention and that it's okay for others to have their spotlight. Learn to be comfortable in the background and respect others' boundaries.

- Work on building empathy: People with NPD often struggle with empathy. Consider how your behavior might affect other people and put yourself in their shoes.

- Remember that change takes time, and progress may be slow.

- Self-compassion: Be kind to yourself when you engage in attention-seeking behaviors, and don't punish yourself too harshly.

- Find alternative ways of getting attention: Instead of always looking for attention from others, try to find ways to give attention to others, such as volunteering or engaging in community service. This can help you feel a sense of purpose and fulfillment.

Therapy can be an important aspect of treatment for attention-seeking behavior. A therapist can help an individual explore the underlying causes of their attention-seeking behavior and develop strategies to overcome it.

Cognitive Behavioral Therapy is a conventional therapy that can be applied to treat attention-seeking behavior. CBT helps people identify and change negative patterns of thinking and behavior. In the case of attention-seeking behavior, a therapist may help an individual recognize and change the thought patterns that lead to attention-seeking behavior, such as thoughts of low self-worth or a need for validation.

Therapy can also help an individual develop healthy coping mechanisms to deal with their underlying issues, such as low self-esteem or anxiety. Moreover, therapy can provide a safe and reliable space for individuals to share their thoughts and feelings without fear of judgment.

It's important to note that changing longstanding behavior patterns can be difficult and may take time and effort. However, it's possible to make progress in addressing attention-seeking behavior with the right support and commitment.

Parents can help their kids as well. Preventing attention-seeking behavior from developing in childhood may involve a combination of strategies. Here are a few that may be helpful:

- Provide positive reinforcement for appropriate behavior: Praise children for making good choices or showing kindness and generosity towards others.

- Set clear boundaries and consequences for negative behavior: Consistently enforce rules and consequences for attention-seeking behavior, such as acting out or being disruptive.

- Teach effective communication skills: Help children learn how to communicate their needs and wants healthily and respectfully.

- Encourage independent play: Give children opportunities to play independently, which can help them develop a sense of self-sufficiency and self-worth.

- Model healthy behavior: Children learn by example, so be mindful of your behavior and try to model healthy ways of seeking attention and validation.

- Encourage children to find other ways of getting attention. For example, by joining a club, sport, or other activities, they're interested in.

- Address underlying emotional or psychological issues: If a child is engaging in attention-seeking behavior because of underlying emotional or psychological issues, it may be beneficial to seek professional counseling or therapy.

Every child is different and may have different needs, so it's important to be patient and understanding when addressing attention-seeking behavior.

Breaking out of this pattern is a big step toward showing that you're vulnerable and humble, and it may feel risky and uncomfortable at first. But if you break out of this pattern, it'll help you move forward and push back against narcissistic patterns that may hurt your relationships with others.

In this chapter, we've examined the issue of attention-seeking behavior and how it can be addressed. Attention-seeking behavior can have negative consequences on one's personal and professional life, and it's crucial to be mindful of the signs of this behavior and take steps to prevent it from becoming a long-term problem. We went over several strategies that can be used to overcome attention-seeking behavior. For example, addressing the underlying causes of this behavior, such as low self-esteem or a need for validation, can help reduce attention-seeking behavior's frequency and intensity. Additionally, being aware of the signs of attention-seeking behavior and learning to recognize when it's happening can help prevent it from becoming a long-term problem. We also highlighted how narcissists might use attention-seeking behavior to manipulate and control others, and it's important to be aware of this dynamic to protect oneself from being manipulated.

In the next chapter, we will talk about how to let go of control. This won't be easy, especially when control has become an ingrained habit. However, learning how to let go of control is important to improve one's relationships and overall well-being. Letting go of control requires patience and practice, but it can be achieved with the right mindset and tools. The chapter will explore why people tend to hold on to control, the benefits of letting go of control, and different strategies that can be used to achieve it.

Chapter 10:
How to Let Go of Control

I n the previous chapter, we saw how attention-seeking, one of the traits of narcissists, can be a major problem in relationships. Another problem that narcissists have is their controlling behavior. Narcissists need to feel in control all the time. They need to feel in charge and that they're making all the decisions. This need for control often manifests itself in controlling behavior.

Controlling behavior in narcissistic relationships can lead to conflict. It can also make the partner feel like they're not in the relationship. This chapter will look at how to let go of the need for control. We'll also look at how to deal with controlling behavior.

Controlling behavior refers to actions or tactics one person uses to exert power and dominance over another, typically in a relationship. These actions may include manipulation, coercion, criticism, isolation, and threats. The goal of controlling behavior is to make the other person dependent on and subservient to the person exhibiting the behavior. It's unhealthy and can lead to serious consequences.

Controlling behavior is often a sign of abuse. Some common signs of control are:

- Inflexibility: The person tries to control every aspect of others' lives, from what to wear to how to spend their free time.

- Need to be in the spotlight: The person may demand all of your attention and may become jealous if not given.

- Being critical and blaming others: The person may constantly criticize others and try to blame others for their problems.

- Being manipulative and crossing boundaries: The person tries to manipulate others emotionally or sexually or may cross physical boundaries without their consent.

- Using guilt trips: The person tries to guilt others into doing what they want or may try to make others feel guilty for their actions

- Being unpredictable: The person is unpredictable in moods or behaviors.

- Making subtle negative jokes: The person may make jokes that put others down or make others feel bad about themselves.

- Keeping score: The person may keep track of who does what in the relationship and may use it to try to control others.

- Crossing the line into abuse: The person may exhibit abusive behavior, such as threats, intimidation, or violence.

Ask yourself and answer honestly; how many of these signs do you exhibit in your daily life?

Whenever controlling behavior makes the other person feel intimidated or afraid, it crosses the line into abuse. The National Domestic Violence Hotline says that abuse is when someone does things to keep power and control over another person. These actions can happen in close relationships, but they can also happen at work, with family, and with friends.

Many types of abuse can involve controlling behavior, such as:

- Physical abuse which is when someone touches another person without their permission and with the intent to hurt them.

- Emotional and verbal abuse includes insulting or threatening someone, following them around all the time, or trying to make them look bad.

- Sexual abuse is when someone is pressured or forced to perform sexual acts against their will.

- Financial abuse is when someone tries to take control of another person's money.

- Digital abuse is when technology, like texting and social media, is used to harass or scare someone.

- Stalking is when someone constantly watches or follows another person, making them feel unsafe.

There may be more than one explanation for controlling behavior. It could be due to:

- Anxiety: Some people deal with anxiety by trying to take charge of certain situations. Treating their anxiety or the condition causing it could make them less controlling.

- Personality disorders: Some personality disorders, like borderline personality disorder and narcissistic personality disorder, may make someone more likely to use controlling behavior.

- Learned behavior: A person may have picked up abusive and controlling behaviors from others. For example, they may have grown up in a home where domestic violence or violence between intimate partners was common, or they may have learned from their parents or other caregivers how to try to control their partner.

We're controlling as adults because there was a time in our childhood when we felt very unsafe. So, I want you to consider thinking back to your childhood and trying to remember when you felt unsafe. Now, look at this from a child's point of view. I'm going to talk about this pattern and how much it hurts. Imagine a child playing on a playground with other kids when, suddenly, another kid starts picking on them. What's the first thing that a child will want to do? They're going to run home to mommy or daddy or whoever takes care of them. It's natural for a child to want to run back to their home, where they're cared for. Home is their safety net. Now, think about how many of us had hard childhoods. If you had a hard childhood, you probably ran home to your mom and dad or your home environment, but your home was also not safe because it was broken somehow. It could be physical abuse, emotional abuse, or just a broken family. Generally, a child can feel unsafe if there's any problem in the family. So, try to see things from the child's point of view. If you're out in the world and feel unsafe, and then go home and still feel unsafe, you should probably stay home. You're stuck, and this is where everything starts. As soon as that sweet, beautiful child starts to feel unsafe in an environment where they should feel safe, many other patterns start to form. If you feel unsafe in your own family, around the people who're supposed to make you feel safe, you'll start to think of ways to protect yourself.

You won't trust the people around you anymore, and you might even stop trusting yourself and your instincts. You then decide to take charge. So basically, your thoughts are "I feel unsafe. I don't trust. I control."

At first, a child growing up in that environment has only two feelings: lack of safety and lack of trust. Eventually, when their personality starts to form, and the ego starts to form, usually between the ages of six and seven, the pattern of not feeling safe gets worse because now the ego starts to make patterns to keep that child safe. Don't forget that they can't trust anyone, not even their family. So, they must depend on themselves. As soon as that ego starts to grow, it tells them, "I'll keep you safe, and I'll keep you safe in this way and that way." This is how we start to think about control, making us very controlling adults. Your ego wants to protect you. So, if you have a controlling personality, you still live in the past in one way or another. You're still living like that little child who didn't feel safe wherever they were.

So now you know why you feel like you're in charge and don't trust life. But how do you get out of this? That's a bit easier. I'll give you tips and tools to help you escape being a control freak and learn how to go with the flow and trust life.

"Letting go of control" refers to relinquishing the need to exert power and influence over others and letting them make their own choices and decisions. It means letting go of the desire to dictate how things should be done and embracing flexibility and openness to different perspectives. It also involves respecting the boundaries of others and not crossing them to achieve one's goals. Letting go of control also means allowing others to be responsible for their own lives and not feeling responsible for their happiness. It's about learning to trust in others and oneself, and ultimately, it's about letting go of the need to control to feel safe and secure.

Here are some simple steps that may help in letting go of control:

1. Recognize and acknowledge the desire to control: The first step in letting go of control is to recognize when you're trying to control a situation or a person. Recognize the triggers that make you want to control and acknowledge the feeling.

2. Understand the underlying cause: Controlling behavior often stems from fears or insecurities. Take some time to explore what may be driving your behavior. It could be fear of rejection, abandonment, or a lack of trust.

3. Practice mindfulness: Mindfulness can help you become more aware of your thoughts, feelings, and actions in the present moment. This can help you identify when you're trying to control something, and instead, pause and take a moment to evaluate the situation.

4. Communicate effectively: Expressing your thoughts, feelings, and needs clearly and assertively is essential in any relationship. Instead of trying to control a situation, learn to communicate effectively to achieve a compromise.

5. Set boundaries: Setting boundaries is important for maintaining control over your life. It means being clear about what you will and will not tolerate and communicating those boundaries to others.

6. Learn to compromise: Letting go of control means learning to compromise and finding a middle ground. The key is to be open to other perspectives and ideas and to work together to find mutually beneficial solutions.

7. Learn to trust: Trusting others and you is key to letting go of control. It means believing in the ability of others to make decisions and trusting that things will work out.

8. Don't worry about being right: The need to control often comes from trying to be right. Being open to different perspectives is the key to letting go of control and the need to always be right.

9. Practice self-care and self-compassion: Taking care of yourself and being kind and compassionate toward yourself can help reduce feelings of anxiety and insecurity, which can be a root of control.

10. Seek help: If you find that your controlling behavior is causing problems in your relationships, it may be a good idea to seek the help of a therapist or counselor. They can help you work through the underlying issues causing your behavior and provide you with tools to manage it more effectively.

11. Be patient with yourself: Changing a long-standing behavior takes time and effort. Be patient with yourself and understand that progress may be slow. Remember that progress is progress and is better than not making any progress.

When we try to influence or control other people, we almost always end up causing conflict and resentment, which makes it hard to get close to them. And it doesn't matter if our intentions are good. Moreover, when we try to change people, we're telling them that they're not "good enough," which makes them less likely to open up to us. Remember that letting go of control is a process that takes time and patience. It also requires a willingness to change and to take responsibility for one's actions. Take very small steps. Remember that if you've had these habits for years or even decades, you can't just wake up one day and say, "Wow, I'm totally trusting, and I don't have any control issues anymore."

Some additional tips I would like to share with you are:

- Learn to give tasks and responsibilities to others instead of thinking that no one can do a job as well as you.

- Curb criticism of others and learn to appreciate and be happy with the efforts of others.

- Consider others' opinions and acknowledge that your stance may not always be the only right one.

- Stop being pushy and be more flexible and open to other people's ideas.

- Loosen up on your schedule and build more margin into your days to allow for the unexpected.

- Learn to be more patient with others, especially your spouse, children, and family.

- Find ways to reduce anxiety levels and learn to relax.

- Learn to go with the flow and not overreact to disruptions in the expected order of things.

- Drop perfectionism and learn to be satisfied with something complete and good.

- Count your blessings, take time to appreciate the positive aspects of your life, and convey gratitude to those around you.

In relationships, problems will arise and it can be easy to get caught up in anxiety, anger, and frustration. However, there are several ways to manage these emotions and stay present. One way to bring yourself into the present moment is by focusing on your breathing. Another way is by stepping away from the situation before reacting, giving yourself a few minutes to think about why you're reacting so negatively. Positive self-talk can also help calm down and manage negative emotions. Remind yourself of things you control, such as your body, reactions, and perception. Another important aspect of living in the present is accepting that you can't control the outcome of every situation. It's important to remind yourself that no matter what the outcome is, you'll be okay.

In romantic relationships, trusting your partner is a vital part of living in the present. Instead of being right, focus on listening to your partner and understanding their viewpoint. Please give them the benefit of the doubt and manage your expectations. Jealousy can also cause problems in a relationship, but it's important to figure out the source of these feelings. Often jealousy results from your insecurities and not from your partner's actions. Forgiving your partner and moving forward together is crucial. If something happened in the relationship that you're battling to let go of, be willing to forgive and move forward. If you're having trouble letting go, consider talking to a therapist for help.

Letting go of control is important for improving relationships, personal growth, autonomy, stress management, mental well-being, and self-awareness. It allows for a more fulfilling and balanced life. Letting go of control:

- Improves relationships: When you let go of control, you allow others to have their thoughts, feelings, and opinions. This allows for healthier communication and deeper understanding in relationships.

- Increases personal growth: When you let go of control, you open yourself up to new experiences, perspectives, and opportunities for personal growth. It allows you to step out of your comfort zone and learn from the experiences of others.

106

- Promotes autonomy: Letting go of control allows others to make their own choices, which promotes autonomy and self-reliance. It also allows you to control your own life and make choices that align with your values and beliefs.

- Reduces stress: Constantly trying to control every aspect of your life can be stressful and draining. Letting go of control can reduce stress and anxiety by allowing you to let go of the need to micromanage every situation.

- Improves mental well-being: Letting go of control can improve mental well-being by reducing feelings of anxiety and insecurity, which are often at the root of control issues. It also helps to develop self-compassion and self-care.

- Increases self-awareness: When you let go of control, you become more self-aware. You start to notice your thoughts, feelings, and actions more clearly. This awareness can help you understand why you need control and how to change that pattern

In conclusion, learning to let go of control and avoiding attention-seeking behavior is crucial for building healthy relationships and personal growth. Paying attention to and showing empathy for the people in our lives is one of the best ways to do this. Having empathy means being able to understand and share other people's feelings. It means giving people our full attention, showing that we care about their lives, and trying to see things from their perspective. By focusing on empathy, we can become the best version of ourselves and create deeper connections with those around us. Empathy can help us create happier and more fulfilling lives. In the next chapter, we will explore together how to build empathy skills.

Chapter 11:
What a Narcissist Can Do to Build Empathy Skills

E mpathy is a crucial aspect of emotional and social development and is one of the main reasons you should help others in need. It's the "capacity to feel or imagine another person's emotional experience" in the most literal sense (McDonald & Messinger, 2011).

People used to believe that young children didn't acquire empathy, but studies on how they react when they see others in agony have proven that this isn't the case. Based on research from the University of Miami, below are some of the phases of growth and factors that influence empathy:

- Newborns: Newborns frequently scream when they hear other babies cry. Reflexive sobbing is also known as emotional contagion. Their behavior doesn't appear to be a mindless reaction to noise but rather an indication of empathy and sensitivity to the negative feelings of others.

- Babies: Babies are concerned about their surroundings. However, as every parent knows, they have difficulty controlling their emotions and are frequently overwhelmed by how other people feel.

- Toddlers: Between the ages of 14 and 36 months, children demonstrate clear indicators of the emotional components of empathy, such as apologizing, caring about others, and offering assistance.

- Early childhood: When children start school, they envision what it's like to be them, not only how other people feel. This is known as the "theory of mind" by psychologists and philosophers. It implies that individuals begin to perceive themselves and others regarding emotions, feelings, and desires.

- From middle childhood to adulthood: Empathy develops dramatically from middle childhood to adulthood, and these changes are part of a greater trait of being compassionate to others. Early prosocial conduct, such as caring for others and seeing things from their perspective, drives helping behavior.

A variety of factors contribute to the early and rapid development of empathy:

- Genetic: Twin studies have repeatedly demonstrated that genes significantly impact how empathy develops, accounting for one-third and one-half of the differences between children.

- Neurodevelopmental factors: Mirror neurons, which are found in both animal and human brains and reflect other people's emotions, could be a mechanism for our brains to connect the experiences of others to our own.

- Temperament: Our personalities play an important role in how we learn to care for others. For example, fearful and shy children appear less inclined to demonstrate empathy in novel situations.

- Mimicry and imitation: Facial mimicry appears to be tied to taking on the emotions of others and begins when a child is very young.

- Parenting: Parents and other caregivers significantly influence how early children learn to interact with others, which influences their ability to feel empathy. As a child, more matching behaviors during play resulted in more empathy. Other research has found that the interaction between a parent and a child is critical for developing empathy in the youngster. This is likely due to the child's sense of safety and affection in the relationship.

Even if the list above isn't exhaustive, it demonstrates how complex and crucial empathy is. Daniel Goleman, a New York Times science correspondent, published *Emotional Intelligence: Why It Can Matter More Than IQ* in 2006. In it, he describes empathy as the ability to "understand how another person feels," and it "comes into play in a broad range of life areas, from sales and management to romance and parenting to compassion and political engagement." We can tell how someone feels by observing their body language, tone of speech, and facial expressions. And there are numerous advantages.

The way we comprehend others affects many aspects of our lives. Here are a few of them:

- How we identify ourselves and how others perceive us: Understanding other people's feelings make us more outgoing and popular as children and adults.

- Positive benefits on work relationships: According to research, having greater empathy improves how well we do our jobs, making us better employees and supervisors.

- Partner empathy was a strong predictor of whether or not the couple would have a happy marriage.

- Improved parenting: Empathy makes parents stronger and more capable of dealing with the problems of raising children.

- Preventing a global disaster: Even though we're programmed to care for those closest to us, if we show compassion to more people, we'll be able to deal with the difficulties that lie ahead, such as global warming, pandemics, and war.

Narcissism is often thought to be characterized by a lack of empathy. In the Diagnostic and Statistical Manual of Mental Disorders of the American Psychiatric Association, one criterion for a formal psychiatric diagnosis of NPD is "lack of empathy."

However, this description comes with an important caveat: "is unwilling to recognize or connect with the feelings and needs of others." It's not the same as not being able to understand what someone else is going through if you don't want to. The idea that a person could feel empathy but doesn't show it may help us understand the personality traits of people we call narcissistic.

Empathy can be both a mental process (being able to understand another person's point of view regarding what they're thinking or feeling) and a physical process (feeling the same emotions as another person). Some researchers have found that the cognitive parts of empathy, like being able to play a role or see things from someone else's point of view, happen in a different part of the brain than the emotional parts.

Our ability to understand and care for others isn't fixed; it may be developed. Making even minor changes in our everyday life can significantly impact our ability to comprehend and care for others. We should teach ourselves how to. I think that people who believe they're narcissistic are not always right. However, some people have been told so many times by other narcissistic people that they begin to believe it. And, because most people whom narcissists have harmed are nearly overly sensitive, they're afraid of harming others.

Walking around with a narcissistic personality is quite unhealthy because you live an angry life, and you feel continuously threatened and unsafe. It's not a pleasant way to live. If you believe you might be a narcissist, consider seeking a mental health professional.

This book will teach you how to change if you believe you're narcissistic. My first piece of advice to you is to quit putting others down. You may say that you try hard, but that's not in your control. I would answer that you could at least aim for 75% if you can't hit 100%. Let me assure you that it will make a significant difference in your life and the lives of others.

In the domain of narcissism, empathy is regarded as a bad bet, but let's define empathy from a psychological standpoint. It's about caring about what other people are going through and considering how our actions or feelings may hurt them. Compassion, generosity, self-awareness, and getting along with people are all linked to empathy.

Now, empathy and sympathy are not synonymous. You show sympathy when you comprehend that someone else is enduring a difficult time or is in pain. For example, when someone suffers a loss or illness, empathy considers the positive and negative things that person has gone through. It's not just about the agony. That is the pity sensation. Empathy is related to emotional intelligence and the ability to understand and respond to what another person is going through.

I firmly believe that you don't have to be in someone else's shoes to comprehend what they're going through. I agree that it can be a little more difficult. However, if we know that an individual is struggling, we can feel empathy for them. We can listen to them and be there for them without discussing our concerns. And be aware that they may not be as readily available as usual. We understand their grief, but we haven't been through it ourselves.

I must tell you one thing: narcissistic persons don't lack empathy; they can experience empathy. It's not as if their brains are missing a chip that wasn't installed when their hardware was built. They have "variable empathy," which means that their baggage, emotions, and needs come in the way of being there for others when they're needed. This suggests that empathy in narcissism is about getting along rather than experiencing empathy.

So, how do you enhance your ability to care for others if you're narcissistic?

- Learn to pay close attention to the details of the people you encounter. Spend time with people you don't know well and ask about them, their lives, and how they're doing. Pay attention to what people from different religious, cultural, and political backgrounds say on social media. Be there for someone when you talk to them. Discover what makes someone angry, joyful, or sad. Meet the locals and learn about their way of life as you travel to new destinations.

- Get out of your comfort zone. Experience something new or visit a different location. Force yourself out of your comfort zone and try to absorb those feelings. Feel what it's like to be unable to do something or unsure how to act. Reach out for assistance. Accept that you may feel helpless sometimes, and don't allow it to make you feel bad. Being modest might help you better understand others. You must be interested in the other person.

- You can't be empathic only to get by, as in, "Oh, you just have to do this empathy thing to get to the other side," or because you want anything from the other person. Empathy is founded on concern for the other person. And if you can't get there, it suggests you need more therapy than this book can provide. It would be best to determine what mental blockages you have and what lessons you learned or didn't learn about caring for others as a child. These issues can be discussed in treatment.

- Request input from friends, family, and coworkers on how well you listen, connect with people, and be open to constructive criticism. We all have biases that make it difficult to understand others. We unconsciously judge others depending on how they look and act. Find ways to interact with people from various locations. Discuss with others the issues that are important to them. Take an interest in your disagreements without passing judgment on them. Donate money to a charity that assists people in other countries.

- Pay attention and be available to others. When someone is talking, don't play with your phone, stare off into the distance, or watch TV. Listen, make eye contact (not creepy eye contact), be present, ask questions, and be curious. Letting someone know you heard and understand their sentiments can help them feel supported, cared for, and understood.

- Always try to put yourself in other people's shoes. Discover what life is like in different areas. How do they work, live, and interact? Spend time with them and try to comprehend their problems. What brings them joy? What do they want? Make friends with people you see frequently but rarely talk to.

- Working on community projects together has been demonstrated in studies to help bring people together and eliminate biases. Find a community project in your own or another country. Join others who've been through similar experiences. Join a group of people from various backgrounds to assist at school, political, or church events.

- Try to read as much as possible about as many different topics as possible. Reading about people's lives from various backgrounds in fiction, nonfiction, newspapers, journals, and online information helps you enhance your emotional intelligence and empathy. Look for authors who have interesting things to say. Learn about their characters' lives, emotions, and thoughts.

- Above all, please don't make it all about you. It doesn't always come back to you. Maintain your attention on them. So many narcissists make the mistake of immediately turning someone else's suffering against them.

Empathy doesn't entail fixing problems. Fixing something allows you to avoid dealing with how you feel about something. Most problems that necessitate empathy are difficult to resolve. They must be addressed.

People with narcissistic personalities don't know how to deal with their emotions, and the remedy is "learning how to do so." In hard times, people want someone to listen to them and be there for them. Narcissistic people may respond, "Oh, no, no, I've got this, I know a guy, I have a connection, I can call this person, I can call that person, I can make this happen." Narcissists will try their best to fix the problem and prove that this wasn't hard. Often, when faced with a problem, we become so fixated on finding a solution that we neglect to consider the emotional impact it may have. It's important to remember that every situation has a psychological component, and addressing the emotions can lead to a more comprehensive and effective resolution. Nothing beats empathy when someone needs to feel a sense of connection and understanding. In the long run, that "fixed problem" may prove beneficial: However, empathy means being present in that time with them. And being with someone else's uncomfortable feelings provides us a chance to look into ourselves and find our feelings and emotions. If you believe you're narcissistic, you must research what impedes your ability to care about others.

Jumping to our next topic, research shows that lack of empathy and lying are closely related. Individuals who lack empathy are more likely to engage in lying behavior. They fail to see the influence of their actions on others and thus don't consider the consequences of their lies. This lack of consideration for others can lead to a lack of remorse or guilt for the harm caused by their lies. Furthermore, people lacking empathy may not understand the importance of honesty in relationships. This can cause significant damage to personal and professional relationships and ultimately make it harder for the liar to build and maintain trust.

Pathological lying, a chronic and excessive lying behavior, is a symptom of several personality disorders, including NPD. In the next chapter, we will delve deeper into the connection between pathological lying and personality disorders and how individuals with these disorders can learn to manage and overcome their lying behavior.

Chapter 13:
How to Stop Compulsive Lying

C laire had been deceiving people since she was a child. She lied about knowing renowned people she didn't know and winning the lottery that she hadn't won. She recently informed everyone at work that she was dying from cancer. As a result, many people felt sorry for her and paid attention to her. She was also allowed to take frequent breaks from work. After being discovered, she got fired. She was fortunate that she was not sued. "I'm not cheating on or stealing from anyone," she told her therapist, whom she's been seeing lately. Claire believed she had lost all her family and friends. No one was hiring her. She was desperate to stop lying, and she thought a therapist could help with that.

Do you also lie? Lying all the time and being excellent at diplomacy are characteristics of NPD.

Narcissists see other people as things, believing they have the right to utilize them. Lying is an essential aspect of dealing with impressions and mirroring. Lies enable narcissists to provide a false image of themselves to potential prey. Those who're attacked lose their ability to make safe and wise decisions. They enter these partnerships unaware of how deadly they are. Once their targets are hooked, narcissists continue to use lies and some truth in various ways to keep their targets "playing."

They deceive by dodging questions and failing to tell the truth. They lie as gaslighting to continually make their targets question themselves and gain more influence over them. They frequently state that they "love" the people they're after. And sometimes, they lie for no apparent reason.

Narcissists are incredibly good at lying and are quite convincing when they do. They enjoy lying because they lack the typical range of human emotions. They're bored because they have nothing to do. They're unconcerned about other people and have no shame or regret. This feeling of emptiness they have also makes lying easy for them. They can look someone in the eyes and lie swiftly and without feeling bad, even when confronted with difficult questions or presented with evidence of lying. It's also simple for them to dispute the lies, make up reasons, and blame others for their behavior, which is also a lie.

They lie to make people feel sorry for them. Because they're exploiters, they exploit people's innate desire to help and care for others. They invent many fictitious ailments and issues based on lies and, sometimes, a smidgeon of truth. Pity plays sometimes feature phony illnesses and injuries, "crazy" ex-boyfriends or girlfriends, car accidents, and theft.

Let me introduce you in more detail to the term pathological lying. This term is often used interchangeably with "compulsive lying," and there's no clear clinical difference between them. Research suggests that compulsive lying falls under the broader definition of pathological lying. Compulsive or pathological lying is a condition in which a person tells lies frequently and compulsively, often without a clear motive or benefit. The lies may be trivial or grandiose and may be told to family members, friends, or strangers. People with compulsive lying often have difficulty controlling their lying and may experience significant distress or impairment in their personal and professional lives because of their behavior. The exact causes of compulsive lying are unknown, but it's thought to be related to biological, psychological, and social factors.

Let me clarify: I'm not referring to inadvertent lying or cognitive dissonance, which occurs when we lie to ourselves. I'm talking about compulsive and intentional lying, which puts you in problems when caught. If this is a problem you face, you can take steps to prevent the compulsive liar in you from surfacing. But first, consider what drives compulsive lying.

Claire lied to attract attention and make herself feel unique. She frequently pretended to be ill to gain immediate attention. This is known as Munchausen's syndrome; a situation in which a person claims to have a disease, illness, or injury to obtain money or other people's attention. When her younger siblings arrived, she felt pushed out of the family. She had been deceiving her classmates and parents since she was a child. Sometimes people might lie to make themselves seem better or more important to control others. They may pretend to have more power or influence than they do and use that to control people. This might be because they don't feel good enough about themselves or because they have too much confidence.

The pathological narcissist liar is dishonest, manipulative, deceitful, and brutal in getting to the heart of a victim's anxieties. They begin by fabricating information about themselves. Then they lie about their exes, employment, and other activities. They lie about their feelings and emotions for you to get close to them quickly. In the end, they'll disparage you and label you as insane. You can be certain that they'll lie about the lying. They will try to justify their actions even if you show them evidence that they were lying.

Why do narcissists usually tell lies?

- They lie to make themselves feel better.

- They lie to harm other people.

- They strive to make it appear that they're superior to the other person by exaggerating the truth.

- When narcissists lie, they attempt to appear as the boss. They lie to benefit themselves because they believe it'll make them appear smarter than the person they're deceiving. Lying also feeds their disorder because they have a victim to lie to. They receive a thrill or hit when they lie to others, making them feel good about themselves.

- Lying is frequently used by the NPD to prepare to gaslight someone. Some people employ gaslighting to keep someone's emotions off-kilter. People wonder if they're crazy when they lie to them face-to-face about what happened. When the victim shows the narcissist evidence of wrongdoing, they will tell them, "You're lying, not me." The narcissist won't only lie and claim that it didn't happen, but they may also attack. This is where the deception begins. They will attempt to portray the victim as the villain.

Do you want to stop lying? Here are some steps to follow to avoid becoming entangled in your web:

1. Ask yourself. What am I not doing right? I always have difficulty telling the truth. Am I a serial liar? Be honest with yourself. I'm not talking about the simple things most of us do daily, like "How are you doing? Fine" while preparing to leap in front of a tram. So, first and foremost, remain true to yourself regardless of what

others do. Lying is difficult because you must remember so much; no matter how intricate you try to be, you'll eventually get caught. As Mark Twain said, "If you tell the truth, you don't have to remember anything." Your life will immediately become less stressful if you stop lying.

Lying is ineffective in the long run. You won't be taken seriously if you're a habitual liar and may never be trusted again. Remember what happened to the child who cried wolf: the truth always comes out.

2. Take care of your emotional needs to stop lying. Many people's activities are unwittingly motivated by the need to satisfy their emotional demands. We all want safety and security, attention from others, significance in life, excitement, intimacy, love, connection to others, self-esteem, and so on, but why lie to get them? Consider occasions when you frequently lied, even when the lies seemed to come from nowhere. What made you tell a lie? Desire to be part of the group, being well thought of and appreciated, and even craving excitement. Consider the rationale and the need that was being addressed.

Lying to meet your basic requirements is stealing. It's also stealing to seek affection, respect, or self-esteem without putting in real labor. Consider genuine ways to meet your desires for self-importance, security, or whatever else you've been pursuing all along, and utilize those as the foundation for your interactions with others.

3. A helpful process is self-hypnosis. Self-hypnosis can help you stop lying by using visualization, positive affirmations, and suggestion to change your subconscious thoughts and behaviors. To stop lying using self-hypnosis, follow these steps:

   a) Make sure you choose a quiet and comfortable place where you won't be disturbed.

   b) To relax your body and mind, close your eyes and take a few deep breaths.

119

c) Visualize a scenario where you tell the truth and how good it feels to be honest.

d) Repeat a positive affirmation to yourself, such as "I'm truthful and honest in all my actions and words."

e) Tell yourself "From now on, I will speak the truth at all times."

f) Allow yourself to drift deeper into hypnosis and imagine yourself living your life as an honest person.

g) When you feel relaxed and calm, count yourself back to full awareness and open your eyes.

h) Repeat this process as often as needed.

It's important to note that self-hypnosis isn't a magic solution; it's a tool to help you change your subconscious thoughts and behaviors. It should be combined with other methods, such as therapy and self-reflection, to address the underlying causes of your lying.

4. Stop and pay attention to what's happening inside the next time you find yourself uttering a lie. Consider your current situation.

- What are you doing?

- What are your thoughts?

- What is your motive for lying? Do you want to feel better or avoid upsetting someone?

By answering these questions, you can learn what conditions, feelings, or other factors cause you to lie. Once you've found certain triggers, examine them carefully and consider different methods to respond to them. When you know you'll be under pressure, plan out possible responses before you get into situations where you may be forced to lie. Work with a therapist to identify the situations, emotions, or thoughts that trigger your lying.

You might be able to figure out why you lie if you can figure out what kind of falsehoods you tell. Perhaps you lie about your work performance because you believe you're not as good as your colleagues. Or perhaps you don't inform your spouse about lunch with an ex because you're terrified of what they'll think, even though you have no intention of cheating. Lying is a complex activity that can be employed in various ways. Most of the time, it serves little purpose in the long run.

If you find it difficult, to be honest with others or yourself, you should consult a mental health expert to figure out what the problem is. However, treatment might be difficult for compulsive liars since they have little control over how much they lie. Instead of discussing the real issue, they may lie to the therapist. A therapist or counselor specializing in treating compulsive lying can help you understand the underlying causes of your behavior and develop strategies to change it.

- Cognitive behavioral therapy is commonly used to treat compulsive lying. It aims to help individuals identify and change the thoughts and behaviors contributing to their lying. The therapist will work with the individual to identify triggers for lying and develop strategies to manage those triggers.

- Medications such as antidepressants, mood stabilizers, and antipsychotics may also be used to treat compulsive lying in some cases. These medications can help reduce anxiety and impulsivity symptoms, which may contribute to compulsive lying.

Some other measures that can be taken to control the habit of lying are:

- Practice honesty: Commit to being truthful in your interactions with others. This can be hard at first, but being honest will become more natural over time.

- Don't lie to prevent a negative outcome: Don't make excuses when you make a mistake. Instead, acknowledge what you did honestly. Accept responsibility by apologizing and resolving the issue as efficiently as you can.

121

- Avoid believing your lies: A difficult truth can be hard to accept. It may be easier to tell yourself that everything is fine. You must be honest about things you don't want to admit to find a solution and avoid lying to yourself (and others). When you reflect honestly on your behavior, you can heal and prevent making the same mistakes in the future. You won't get anywhere by lying.

- Make sure you don't miss any key details: In this case, you're lying by omission. Don't omit details or hide any aspects of the story from someone when talking to them.

- Learn new communication skills: A therapist can teach you new ways to communicate effectively and assertively without lying.

- It's not necessary to lie to impress people: You may be tempted to exaggerate if you feel like you're not good enough the way you are. Instead of lying, remind yourself of your positive traits. It's important to emphasize these things, not lies that may temporarily impress people.

- Address underlying issues: Pathological lying may be a symptom of deeply rooted mental health issues such as anxiety, depression, or personality disorders, which can be addressed by therapy and medication.

- Build a support system: Surround yourself with people who will support and encourage you as you work to change your behavior.

- Be patient and persistent: Changing compulsive lying is a difficult process that can take time and effort, so it's important to be patient and persistent in your efforts to change. Remember that setbacks are normal and you should not give up on treatment.

- It's imperative to acknowledge when you lie to stop doing it: Reflect on why you told the lies you told throughout the day. By doing this, you can better understand what motivates you to lie, including insecurity or the desire to please others. Taking the time to reflect honestly can be incredibly therapeutic. Journaling can be a safe space to process your emotions and learn from them.

Remember that healing and change require time, effort, and professional help. The right treatment and support can overcome compulsive lying and improve your overall well-being.

Here I want to point out a very important factor that can hinder a narcissist from improving and overcoming the habit of pathological lying; emotional dysregulation. Emotional dysregulation refers to difficulty controlling one's emotions, resulting in intense or unstable emotional reactions disproportionate to the situation. It can present itself in various ways, such as feeling overwhelmed by emotions, having difficulty managing anger or sadness, or experiencing rapid mood swings.

When emotionally dysregulated, people may struggle to focus on long-term goals or plans and may be more likely to give in to immediate impulses or desires, even if they know that these actions are not in their best interest. They may also have a harder time regulating their emotions in response to stressors or triggers, which can lead to feelings of helplessness or hopelessness.

Emotional dysregulation is a common symptom among individuals with NPD. However, just like lying, emotional dysregulation is treatable. More information on treating emotional dysregulation can be found in the next chapter.

Chapter 14:
What Is Emotional Dysregulation?

T he objective of this book is to focus on the most challenging ways individuals communicate with one another and to provide you with advice on how to deal with these patterns in yourself. It'll be better for those around you and much better for you. We've covered a wide variety of topics in earlier chapters, mostly the problems narcissism frequently causes for others. So, let's speak about one of the most important aspects of narcissism: the inability to control emotions.

So, what is emotional dysregulation? Emotional dysregulation refers to difficulty managing or controlling emotions. This can manifest in different ways, such as feeling overwhelmed by emotions, having intense or unstable emotions, or having difficulty healthily expressing emotions. Emotional dysregulation can indicate a mental health condition or it can occur because of trauma or other life experiences. Emotional dysregulation occurs when emotions are not well-regulated and don't fall within the range of usual emotional responses.

A person's emotional regulation is initiating, inhibiting, and modulating their mental state and behavior in response to external or internal stimuli. Here's how it works:

1. There are many ways an event can trigger a subjective experience (emotion or feeling), whether internal or external (thinking about something sad or encountering an angry person).

2. It's followed by a cognitive response (thoughts) and an emotional-related physiological response (for example, increased heart rate).

3. It's immediately followed by an action or expression (avoidance, physical action, etc.).

To be emotionally regulated, one must maintain a socially acceptable level of thoughts, behaviors, and expressions.

Dysregulation can also refer to mood swings or emotional instability. Anger, sadness, irritability, frustration, and anger are all possible emotions involved. Even though most people think of emotional dysregulation as a childhood issue that resolves as a child acquires better emotional regulation skills and strategies, this problem may persist into adulthood if not addressed. It's common for these individuals to struggle with emotional dysregulation throughout their lives, resulting in interpersonal problems, academic problems, and difficulty functioning in the workplace.

A fundamental aspect of dysregulation is impulsivity, which occurs when a person acts without considering the consequences. Throwing something when angry is usually considered a habit, but it's also a form of impulsivity due to emotional dysregulation. Narcissists often engage in this behavior verbally, speaking whatever comes to mind, no matter how hurtful, without thinking about the consequences. Verbal also includes texting, emailing, or other unfiltered communication.

Any person under the effect of impulsivity may become enraged and hurts others. When a person is angry, depressed, anxious, or impetuous, they may act out of proportion. Overreacting is one of the hallmarks of narcissism.

The symptoms of emotional dysregulation can vary depending on the individual and the condition's underlying cause. However, some common symptoms of emotional dysregulation include:

- Intense or unstable emotions: The person may experience sudden and intense changes in mood, such as going from feeling calm to feeling extremely angry or anxious in a short period.

- Difficulty managing emotions: The person may have trouble regulating their emotions and may find it hard to calm down once upset. They may also have trouble recognizing or labeling their emotions.

- Difficulty expressing emotions: The person may have trouble healthily expressing their emotions and may resort to self-harm, substance abuse, or other harmful behaviors to cope.

- Impulsivity: The person may act impulsively without thinking about the consequences of their actions.

- Difficulty maintaining relationships: The person may have trouble maintaining stable relationships due to intense or unstable emotions and impulsive behavior.

- Emotionally reactive: The person may overreact emotionally to small incidents.

- Chronic feelings of emptiness: The person may have a

  sense of emptiness or a feeling of not having any sense of self.

It's important to note that these symptoms may also be symptoms of other mental health conditions, such as borderline personality disorder or bipolar disorder, so a proper evaluation by a mental health professional is necessary for a diagnosis.

So, what causes emotional dysregulation? The exact cause of emotional dysregulation isn't fully recognized, but it's thought to be a blend of genetic, biological, and environmental factors. Some possible causes of emotional dysregulation include:

- Genetics: Studies have suggested that emotional dysregulation may have a genetic component. Individuals with a family history of mental health conditions such as borderline personality disorder or bipolar disorder may be at a higher risk of developing emotional dysregulation.

- Brain chemistry: Imbalances in certain chemicals in the brain, such as serotonin and dopamine, may play a role in the development of emotional dysregulation.

- Trauma: Trauma, such as childhood abuse or neglect, can cause emotional dysregulation.

- Environment: Growing up in a chaotic or unstable environment can lead to emotional dysregulation.

- Medical conditions: Some conditions, such as thyroid disorders or chronic pain, may also contribute to emotional dysregulation.

- Developmental disorders: Below is a list of the disorders most commonly associated with emotional dysregulation:

- Narcissistic personality disorder
- Attention-deficit hyperactivity disorder
- Autism spectrum disorders
- Bipolar disorder
- Borderline personality disorder
- Complex post-traumatic stress disorder
- Disruptive mood dysregulation disorder
- Fetal alcohol syndrome

In the context of mental disorders, emotional dysregulation may be characterized by heightened sensitivity to emotional stimuli and a slower return to a normal emotional state.

The essence of dysregulation is that narcissistic individuals lack an internal thermostat for self-control. They become irritated when things don't go the way they want. If something doesn't go their way, they may lash out instantly and throw a tantrum. If mentally stable persons are triggered, most of these feelings may dissipate on their own, or they're dealt with in ways that don't cause significant impairment. Those dealing with chronic emotional dysregulation become so overwhelmed that they can't properly process their emotions. Mentally stable persons don't immediately get caught in their emotions. They breathe, take a break, and think before acting. They might take a walk. They could consult with a friend. They could take a bath. They may go for a run, but they don't lash out at others to cool down their anger.

With emotional dysregulation, individuals lack awareness of their emotions and are unable to regulate them. They will try to avoid any negative emotions and, when faced with them, tend to lack the ability to solve their emotions independently.

In earlier developmental stages, dysregulation can lead to more intense "growing pains" or "phases." Left untreated, it can precipitate a life-long struggle with family, friends, relationships, and coworkers.

The narcissist may use things from the outside world like drugs or alcohol. They relieve their tension by yelling at others, wasting money on useless things, or seeking approval from others. So, they employ outsiders to make the regulation that should be done internally.

Narcissistic dysregulation and impulsivity are responsible for a major portion of the emotional damage caused by this narcissistic behavior. The instability is what makes narcissistic people frightening. It's what gives people the impression that they're unpredictable. That's why some people shun you and even separate themselves from you. And it's why people are nervous around you and walk on eggshells because they never know what will set you off. So, what you should do is not respond violently when triggered, making people less anxious around you.

Emotional dysregulation can significantly impact a person's daily life, affecting their ability to function in various areas such as relationships, work, and school. Some ways that emotional dysregulation can affect a person's life include:

- Difficulty maintaining relationships: The person may have trouble maintaining stable relationships due to intense or unstable emotions and impulsive behavior.

- Difficulty functioning in school or work: The person may have difficulty completing tasks, meeting deadlines, or maintaining focus due to emotional instability.

- Difficulty with self-care: The person may have trouble caring for themselves physically and emotionally.

- Difficulty with self-esteem: The person may have low self-esteem and feel bad about themselves due to emotional instability.

- Increased risk of self-harm and suicide: The person may be more likely to engage in self-harm or suicidal behavior to cope with their intense emotions.

- Increased risk of substance abuse: The person may be more likely to use drugs or alcohol to cope with intense emotions.

- Difficulty with social interactions: The person may have trouble interacting with others due to emotional instability and impulsivity.

The treatment of emotional dysregulation can vary depending on the individual and the condition's underlying cause. However, some common ways to treat and manage emotional dysregulation include:

- Therapy: Different types of therapy, such as cognitive-behavioral therapy, dialectical behavior therapy, and psychoanalytic therapy, can be effective in helping people with emotional dysregulation learn to manage their emotions and improve their relationships.

- Medication: Antidepressants, mood stabilizers, and antipsychotics may be prescribed to help balance brain chemicals and regulate emotions.

- Mindfulness practices: It's possible to learn how to manage emotions effectively by practicing mindfulness exercises such as meditation, yoga, and deep breathing.

- Support groups: Support groups can provide a safe and supportive environment for people with emotional dysregulation to share their experiences and learn from others.

- Lifestyle changes: Adopting a healthy lifestyle, such as regular exercise, a balanced diet, and adequate sleep, can help improve overall mental and physical health.

- Healthy coping mechanisms: Developing healthy coping mechanisms like journaling, art, or music can provide a positive outlet for managing intense emotions.

- Psychoeducation: Learning about emotions, how they work, and how to manage them through psychoeducation can improve emotional regulation.

Psychiatric treatment and professional psychological counseling are necessary to overcome this condition since emotional regulation is linked to mental health.

Dialectical behavioral therapy is an effective treatment for emotional dysregulation. Patients participating in DBT are taught skills for managing emotions, dealing with conflict, and tolerating uncomfortable feelings as a form of cognitive behavioral therapy. DBT emphasizes mindfulness, which cultivates a sense of awareness and builds self-control. DBT patients practice their newfound skills in one-on-one and group sessions to prepare them for real-life applications. Emotional dysregulation is a complex condition, and treatment should be tailored to individual needs.

A combination of therapy, medication, and lifestyle changes may be necessary for some people, while others may only require one treatment. A proper evaluation by a mental health professional is necessary for a proper diagnosis and treatment plan.

When a parent has emotional dysregulation, they may have difficulty providing a stable and consistent emotional environment for their child. As a result, children can have difficulty regulating their emotions and are at risk of developing emotional dysregulation. For example, a parent with emotional dysregulation might have difficulty remaining calm and composed when their child is upset. This can make it challenging for the child to learn how to calm themselves down in similar situations. Additionally, a parent with emotional dysregulation may struggle to provide emotional support and validation to their child, making it difficult for the child to learn how to regulate their emotions healthily.

Children with emotional dysregulation exhibit symptoms according to their developmental stage. Usually, a child with emotional dysregulation may experience the following:

- A tendency to be defiant

- Problems making and keeping friends

- Problems complying with requests from teachers or parents

- Reduced ability to focus on tasks

Although emotional dysregulation isn't limited to a specific parenting style or family structure and can occur in any family, a parent with emotional dysregulation can still be loving, caring, and supportive. However, they may need additional support and resources to help them manage their emotions and provide their child with a stable and healthy environment.

There are several reasons why it's so crucial for narcissistic parents to learn emotional stability for the sake of their children.

- Emotional stability is crucial for healthy child development. Children need a stable and consistent emotional environment to develop healthy emotional regulation skills. A parent who struggles with emotional dysregulation may not be able to provide this type of environment, which can put the child at risk of developing emotional and behavioral problems.

- A stable emotional environment helps children develop self-esteem and self-worth. Narcissistic parents may tend to be overly critical or demanding of their children, making it difficult for them to build a healthy sense of self-worth.

- Emotional stability helps parents be more effective in their parenting. When parents can healthily regulate their emotions, they're better able to respond to their children's needs in a calm, thoughtful, and appropriate manner. This can help create a positive and nurturing environment for the child.

- Emotionally stable parents can provide a good example for their children. Parents who can model healthy emotional regulation can help their children learn how to regulate their emotions healthily.

Not all narcissists have the same level of malignancy. Some may have traits of it, but not necessarily suffer from the disorder, and that emotional learning stability takes time and effort. Additionally, having a narcissistic parent doesn't mean a child will suffer from emotional dysregulation or other problems. However, it's important for narcissistic parents to be aware of their behavior's impact on their children and to seek help, if necessary, to provide the best possible environment for their children to thrive in.

In this chapter, we've talked about how emotional dysregulation can be caused by various factors such as genetics, brain chemistry, trauma, and environmental factors. One of the key causes of emotional dysregulation is childhood trauma, which can lead to the development of defense mechanisms as coping mechanisms. Defense mechanisms are mental processes that people use to protect themselves from uncomfortable emotions, such as anxiety or guilt. They're unconscious and automatic, which means that a person may not even be aware they're using them.

Common defense mechanisms include repression, denial, and projection. Childhood trauma can affect the emotional regulation of an individual, making them more likely to engage in self-harm or suicidal behavior as a way of coping with their intense emotions.

People with emotional dysregulation who've experienced childhood trauma may develop defense mechanisms to cope with the emotional pain. These defense mechanisms can help relieve emotional distress, but they can also prevent the person from dealing with the underlying issues and thus can be detrimental in the long run. So, in the next chapter, we'll go over the most common defense mechanisms and learn everything about them. Knowing all about them will improve the chances of healing.

Chapter 15:
Understanding Defense Mechanisms

D efense mechanisms are unconscious coping strategies that people use to protect themselves from overwhelming stress, anxiety, or emotional pain. Recognizing and tackling these defense mechanisms can help individuals better understand and manage their emotions. Surprisingly, most people are unaware that these characteristics are often detrimental to their health and seldom attempt to replace them with better ones.

Narcissistic defenses are techniques of retaining the idealized elements of oneself and denying the portions that aren't. They're usually strict and all-encompassing. They're frequently motivated by shame and guilt, whether they realize it or not. To get rid of painful feelings, narcissists usually employ several defenses until they find one that works.

Defense mechanisms can be broadly classified according to their function. They could be classified as:

- Adaptive

- Intermediate/neurotic

- Maladaptive/pathological

Adaptive defense mechanisms are healthy ways that people deal with difficult emotions. Humor, anticipation, and suppression are examples of adaptive defenses. They help a person healthily manage negative feelings and events. For example, if a person feels embarrassed, they may use humor to reduce negative emotions. Adaptive defenses are considered healthy because they can help a person deal with negative situations positively and reduce the negative impact of events. They're associated with good mental health and a positive personality.

Intermediate or neurotic defense mechanisms are ways that people unconsciously deal with emotional pain. These mechanisms aren't as flexible as adaptive defenses, which are healthy ways to cope with stress. Instead, intermediate defenses focus on keeping a person calm and avoiding frustration. For example, if someone feels insulted by a coworker, they may act overly nice to that person the next time they see them to avoid feeling angry. This is an example of "response creation," a type of intermediate defense. These mechanisms can be useful when used correctly, but they don't address the person's true feelings or the root of the problem. They can keep people away from their true emotions and the real causes of their suffering.

Maladaptive defenses are at the other end of the spectrum. These are techniques for keeping potentially hazardous unpleasant emotions away from the self. Maladaptive defenses are primarily employed while dealing with other people. This is because, in contrast to adaptive defenses, which work on an intrapsychic level, maladaptive defenses employ others to (unconsciously) control one's emotional pain. Overusing these protective systems is frequently associated with relationship issues, psychiatric diseases, and personality disorders.

When it comes to people with NPD, the most common defense mechanisms used by a narcissist are:

- Denial: When someone doesn't accept facts or reality to avoid dealing with unpleasant feelings.

- Repression: When someone unconsciously pushes away unpleasant thoughts or memories to forget them.

- Projection: When someone attributes their negative thoughts or feelings to someone else.

- Displacement: When someone redirects their strong feelings or anger towards a safer target.

- Regression: When someone acts or behaves in a way that is associated with a younger age or earlier stage in life.

- Rationalization: When someone justifies their behavior with their own set of facts.

- Sublimation: When someone channels their strong feelings or emotions into an appropriate and safe activity or hobby.

- Minimization: Narcissists may downplay or minimize the importance of events or actions that threaten their self-image.

- Idealization and Devaluation: Narcissists may idealize or idolize certain people or groups while devaluing others who don't align with their self-image.

- Grandiose Fantasy: Narcissists may have unrealistic and grandiose fantasies of themselves and their abilities. They tend to overestimate their talents and capabilities.

- Reaction Formation: When someone acts opposite to their feelings to avoid showing negative emotions.

- Compartmentalization: When someone separates different aspects of their life to avoid dealing with certain issues.

- Intellectualization: During a challenging situation, the person may decide not to respond emotionally but focus on calculable data.

- Splitting: When someone constantly divides people or things into two categories: good and bad.

- Cognitive Dissonance: In cognitive dissonance, two or more contradictory beliefs, attitudes, or values are held simultaneously by a person.

- Dissociation: Pathological narcissism has been compared to dissociative identity disorder (formerly multiple personality disorder)

Studies show that the lack of a consistent sense of self can lead to feelings of shame, sadness, and helplessness. To avoid this, narcissists use defense mechanisms such as altering the meanings of words, denying the existence of negative traits, and idealizing those who support them while devaluing those who don't. These tactics allow them to appear superior to others and maintain a consistent image of themselves, even if it means making others feel bad about themselves.

But the analysis of narcissism's pathologies by Otto Kernberg and Heinz Kohut has helped us better understand how narcissists protect themselves by looking at denial, separation, projective identification, and pathological idealization work. Otto Kernberg and Heinz Kohut were prominent psychoanalysts who developed influential theories on narcissism.

Otto Kernberg, on the other hand, proposed a three-level model of the narcissistic personality, which includes normal narcissism, malignant narcissism, and NPD. He also suggested that individuals with NPD use defense mechanisms such as denial, projection, and idealization to protect their self-esteem and avoid dealing with their feelings of inadequacy. Denial is used to avoid acknowledging or accepting certain aspects of themselves or their behavior that may be viewed as negative. Projection is used to disown their shortcomings by projecting them onto others. Idealization is used to avoid dealing with their feelings of inadequacy by idealizing themselves, romantic partners, or even objects or ideals.

On the other hand, Heinz Kohut developed the self-psychology theory of narcissism, which emphasizes the role of the self in developing NPD. He believed that narcissistic individuals have a fragile sense of self and a lack of self-esteem, which leads them to seek validation and admiration from others to boost their sense of self-worth. He also emphasized that the key to treating narcissistic individuals is to help them develop a more solid and stable sense of self.

Both theories of narcissism have been influential in shaping the understanding of this disorder and how to treat it. Both models have been used in therapy and have effectively treated individuals with NPD.

Below you'll find a more detailed explanation of some of the most common defense mechanisms utilized by narcissists.

1. Denial

This is a basic defense mechanism in which a person refuses to acknowledge or accept an event or reality, causing emotional pain. Denial can be a temporary or a long-lasting response and can be conscious or unconscious. When a person is in denial, they may not be aware of their behavior or the reality of the situation. For example, a person who has lost a loved one may deny that the person has died and continue to believe that the person will return.

Denial can also be used in response to a difficult diagnosis, such as cancer. The person may refuse to accept the diagnosis or the severity of the illness. In some cases, denial can be a healthy response, as it can temporarily allow a person to cope with a traumatic event, but in most cases, it's maladaptive. It can prevent the person from facing reality and seeking help to cope with it.

2. Repression

This mechanism involves consciously or unconsciously suppressing unwanted thoughts, feelings, or memories. It's a way to avoid or reject thoughts or memories that are too painful to deal with.

As a defense mechanism used by a narcissist, repression protects the narcissist's self-image and self-esteem by keeping negative thoughts and feelings about themselves out of their conscious awareness. They might repress the memories of past failures, rejections, or criticisms that could affect their self-esteem, to maintain the illusion of self-grandiosity. They may also repress negative thoughts or feelings about themselves, such as insecurity or vulnerability, to sustain the illusion of being perfect and invulnerable.

While repression can be an effective way for a narcissist to avoid dealing with difficult emotions or memories in the short term, it can be maladaptive in the long term. It can prevent the person from facing reality and seeking help to cope with it. Thinking grandiosely to avoid having the courage to admit one weakness or limitation leads to another defense mechanism known as projection.

3. Projection

This is a defense mechanism in which people attribute their unacceptable or unwanted thoughts, feelings, or behaviors to someone else. This allows them to avoid taking responsibility for their actions and dealing with their own negative emotions or impulses. For example, someone who's angry may accuse others of being angry, someone who's guilty may accuse others of being guilty, someone who's dishonest may accuse others of being dishonest, and so on.

Projection can also be used to maintain a positive self-image. People may project their positive qualities onto others and see these qualities as belonging to others rather than themselves. Projection can also manipulate others by making them feel guilty or responsible for the person's feelings or actions.

It's important to note that projection is often an unconscious defense mechanism, and people may not be aware that they're using it. It's a common defense mechanism found in many different personality types, but it's particularly associated with narcissistic, paranoid, and schizoid personalities.

4. Displacement

    This mechanism involves redirecting feelings or emotions from the source of anxiety or frustration to a less threatening or more acceptable target.

    Narcissists use displacement to protect their self-esteem and self-image by redirecting anger, frustration, and resentment toward people or objects perceived as less significant or threatening. For example, narcissists upset with their boss for criticizing their work may come home and take out their anger on their partner or children, instead of confronting their boss. They may also displace their feelings of inadequacy or failure by blaming someone else for their shortcomings rather than taking responsibility for them. Additionally, narcissists may displace their feelings of vulnerability onto other people or objects instead of facing them directly.

5. Regression

    A defense mechanism triggered by stress and anxiety in which a person engages in primitive or immature behaviors or thinking.

    Narcissists use regression as a defense mechanism to protect their self-image and self-esteem by not taking responsibility for their actions or avoiding difficult emotions. The narcissist, for example, might become demanding, sulky, or pouty instead of accepting responsibility for a difficult decision. Alternatively, they may become impulsive, acting on their immediate desires instead of considering the consequences of their actions. As a means of manipulation or control, they may also act like a helpless child to manipulate or control others.

6. Rationalization

    A mechanism in which people justify their behavior or thoughts using logical and rational explanations, even if they're not entirely true or accurate. This allows them to avoid taking responsibility for their actions or dealing with negative emotions or impulses. For example, someone fired from their job may rationalize it as being due to a lack of opportunity or a poor economy rather than their poor performance or attitude. Someone who cheats on a test may rationalize it as a necessary step to get ahead rather than taking responsibility for their dishonesty.

    Rationalization can also be used to maintain a positive self-image by making excuses for one's negative behavior or thoughts. Rationalization isn't just a defense mechanism; it's also used to restore ego sync and make people accept themselves.

7. Sublimation

    This one involves channeling potentially harmful impulses into constructive or socially acceptable behavior. When narcissism is present, sublimation can refer to using one's sense of self-importance to succeed in one's chosen field rather than engaging in harmful behavior. Narcissists can use sublimation to maintain their self-worth while avoiding negative consequences.

8. Minimization

    Using this mechanism, narcissists downplay events or actions that threaten their self-image or worth. A narcissist can use it to avoid acknowledging and taking responsibility for their own mistakes or flaws. Narcissists often ignore their actions' negative impact by dismissing them as insignificant or unimportant. Also, they might reject criticism or negative feedback as non-relevant or useless. Thus, they maintain their image of perfection or superiority in this way.

    Similarly, a narcissist can minimize problems or conflicts in relationships by downplaying their significance. The issue may be trivialized or dismissed rather than addressed and resolved. By doing this, the narcissist can maintain the relationship on their terms.

9. Idealization

This defense mechanism involves viewing someone as perfect or superior. The narcissist may have an idealized view of a certain individual or group they believe to be powerful, successful, or influential. Also, they may view themselves as superior to others because of their abilities and accomplishments.

10. Devaluation

As opposed to idealization, devaluation refers to viewing someone as less valuable or inferior. Narcissists may devalue those who threaten their self-image or oppose their goals. In addition, they might view their own mistakes or shortcomings as insignificant or trivial. Relationships are no different. At the beginning of an intimate relationship, a narcissist may fantasize about a potential romantic partner. However, as soon as partners fail to meet their expectations, they begin to devalue them, seeing them as inferior or worthless. Eventually, this can lead to a pattern of "idealize, devalue, discard," whereby the narcissist alternates between idealizing and devaluing their partners.

11. Fantasy

This is a coping mechanism that uses imagination to create mental scenarios or narratives detached from reality. People may use fantasy to escape difficult or overwhelming situations, cope with emotional pain, or alleviate stress. Fantasy can also be used to process and make sense of difficult or traumatic experiences. It can be healthy in moderation and balanced with reality-oriented problem-solving.

Narcissists may use fantasy to deal with problems and difficult situations. They may create an idealized image of themselves and their lives in which they're powerful, successful, and admired by others. This idealized self-image can serve as a form of emotional regulation. It can help them temporarily detach from reality and feel more in control.

12. Reaction Formation

This is a tricky defense mechanism in which individuals act opposite to their true feelings to avoid showing negative emotions or dealing with unpleasant or uncomfortable thoughts or impulses. For example, an insecure individual may act very confident and self-assuredly to avoid showing vulnerability or weakness. Or an individual who's feeling angry may act in a very friendly and pleasant manner to avoid expressing anger and potentially damaging relationships.

This defense mechanism is used to avoid dealing with the underlying negative emotions or impulses; instead, they project a different image of themselves than they want to be perceived. They try to avoid negative emotions by masking them with positive emotions and avoiding negative thoughts by hiding them behind a façade.

13. Compartmentalization

This is a defense mechanism used by narcissists to separate different aspects of their life into separate "compartments." This allows them to maintain a positive self-image and avoid taking responsibility for their negative actions, thoughts, and feelings.

By separating different groups of people, the narcissist can maintain the belief that they're a likable and desirable individual while avoiding the uncomfortable realization that their behavior toward some people isn't in line with this self-image.

14. Intellectualization

Also known as isolation, is a defense mechanism that narcissists use to distance themselves emotionally from a distressing situation or event. They use their intellect and reason to avoid taking responsibility for their mistakes or flaws and feeling guilty or ashamed. It's also used to distance themselves from the feelings and emotions of others, seeing them as illogical, to maintain their self-image, and to refrain from empathizing.

15. Splitting

This is a defense mechanism used by narcissists and people with personality disorders like borderline personality disorder to protect themselves from emotional pain. It involves dividing people or things into two separate categories: good and bad. This happens when someone can't understand how two different things about the same object can coexist. This can lead to black-and-white thinking and a lack of nuance in the person's understanding of the situation.

The narcissistic person harbors an all-or-nothing primitive machine, and everything is either bad or good. There's no in-between. There are no gray areas in the world.

16. Cognitive Dissonance

Cognitive dissonance refers to the psychological discomfort or tension that a person experiences when they hold two or more contradictory beliefs, opinions, or values at the same time. This can happen when a person's behavior or actions are inconsistent with their beliefs or values, creating discomfort or unease. For example, a person who smokes cigarettes may experience cognitive dissonance because they know smoking is harmful to their health, but they continue to smoke.

17. Dissociation

This is one of the most complex defense mechanisms. Dissociation is a change in how your mind processes information. You can experience a sense of disconnection from your ideas, emotions, memories, and surroundings. It can affect your sense of identity and your perception of time.

We live a continuous mental existence. Both our internal and external worlds are represented in a seamless motion through memories, perceptions, and representations. We sometimes become disengaged when faced with horror or unbearable truths. We lose sight of space, time, and the continuity of our identity. Our surroundings, incoming information, and circumstances are minimized so that we become someone else without a clear understanding of who we are.

Occasionally, individuals may develop what is known as "dissociative identity disorder."

Several other defense mechanisms can be commonly observed in individuals with narcissistic tendencies. Some of them include the following:

- Gaslighting: Narcissists may manipulate others by denying the reality of certain events or making others question their perception of reality.

- Object Constancy: Narcissists may have difficulty maintaining a positive image of someone when they're not present. They may idealize people when they're around, but when they're not, they might devalue them.

- Magical Thinking: Narcissists may believe that their thoughts or actions can control external events. They may have unrealistic expectations and believe that they're special or unique in some way.

- Projective Identification: Narcissists may project their unwanted thoughts, feelings, or impulses onto others and attribute them to the other person.

- Acting Out: Narcissists may act impulsively and without thinking; they may engage in reckless or dangerous behavior, and they may use drugs, alcohol, or other addictive behaviors to cope with negative emotions.

- Pseudo-Altruism: It can be used as a defense mechanism by the narcissist to present oneself as a kind and caring person while hiding underlying selfish or manipulative motives. For example, a narcissist may offer to help someone with a task, but only if it will benefit them in some way, such as gaining their trust or admiration.

- Anticipation: It's used to gain control over others by planning and strategizing to accomplish their goals. A narcissist may use anticipation to manipulate others and plan for future events. A narcissist may plan for a conflict with a coworker in advance so that they can be in the driving seat.

- Narcissistic Rage: Narcissists may react with anger or rage when their self-image is threatened; they can become very aggressive and even violent to keep their self-worth.

This chapter intends to provide you with a list of common defense mechanisms observed in individuals with narcissistic tendencies. However, keep in mind that defense mechanisms can differ from person to person.

Researchers have found that different types of narcissism (grandiose and vulnerable) are linked to different defense mechanisms. Grandiose narcissism is linked to both healthy and unhealthy defense mechanisms, while vulnerable narcissism is linked to mostly unhealthy defense mechanisms. Grandiose narcissism is significantly associated with anticipation, pseudo-altruism, rationalization, and dissociation. People with grandiose narcissism tend to have less psychological distress, while people with vulnerable narcissism tend to have more.

To understand yourself better, it's important to pay attention to how you react in different situations and your thoughts and feelings at that time. Here are some tips for recognizing and tackling these defense mechanisms:

- Take a break from strong emotional experiences. Give yourself time and space to process and understand your emotions before addressing them.

- Define and name the feelings and needs that are part of strong emotional experiences. Identifying and naming your emotions can help you better understand them.

- Identify and investigate the inner images, sounds, and sensations behind your emotional experiences. Pay attention to your thoughts, feelings, and physical sensations to understand the underlying emotions.

- Find the psychological source of the experience and talk to them. Reflect on past experiences or events that may have contributed to the current emotional experience.

- Don't judge emotional experiences based on how good or bad they are. Emotions are natural and valid, and it's important to accept them without judgment.

- Keep a constructive, non-judgmental attitude about your emotional experience. Approach your emotions with curiosity and openness rather than criticism or self-judgment.

- Think about how fear, shame, guilt, and anger play a part. These emotions can often be triggers for defense mechanisms, and understanding how they contribute to our emotional experiences can help us better address them.

- Defense mechanisms often lead to overreactions or disproportionate responses to stressors. It's important to recognize your defense mechanisms when emotions are out of balance and to address them accordingly.

It's normal to use defense mechanisms as part of our coping mechanisms. It's not always bad, but when it impedes our ability to live our lives or causes distress, it's a sign that we should address them.

At this stage of the book, you've learned a lot of tips and tricks on how to control your narcissistic traits. You could reflect on how the traumas you experienced in your childhood, such as emotional neglect, abandonment, or physical abuse, led you to develop defense mechanisms such as denial, projection, and idealization to protect your self-esteem and avoid dealing with your feelings of inadequacy. You may have realized how these defense mechanisms contributed to your narcissistic traits and behaviors.

As you're reaching the end of the book, you may feel ready to take the next step and begin the healing process. The book's final chapter could offer highly effective steps for healing, such as therapy, self-reflection, and practicing self-compassion, that can help the individual better understand and manage their emotions and form healthier relationships with others.

Chapter 16:
Highly Effective Steps Toward Healing

T his is the last chapter of the book and it's time to review the key points we've covered in each chapter. This will help solidify the main concepts and themes that were discussed throughout the book. We will go over the main points, highlighting the most important information.

NPD characteristics include an inflated sense of haughtiness, a lack of empathy for others, and a need for admiration and approval. Narcissistic individuals often have a grandiose sense of self, a strong need for attention, and an excessive desire for power and control. They may have difficulty maintaining healthy relationships and engage in manipulative and exploitative behavior toward others.

But is it possible to get rid of narcissism? Most people think that there's no treatment for narcissism, but for a narcissist to get better, they must WANT to change. Even with wanting to change, it's still a very hard fight.

While it's not easy to change narcissistic behavior, it's possible with the help of therapy and self-reflection.

Understanding the Causes of Narcissism

Narcissism is believed to be caused by genetic and environmental factors.

Childhood trauma and experiences, such as neglect or abuse, can play a significant role in developing narcissistic traits. If a child grows up in circumstances where their needs are not met or are consistently invalidated, they may develop a sense of insecurity and need constant validation from others. Abuse and trauma can lead to the development of narcissistic traits in a child by causing them to form an "inner child" that's overly self-centered and entitled, as well as a "shadow self" that's deeply ashamed and insecure.

This can happen because the child, to cope with the abuse and trauma, may dissociate from their true self and create a false self that's focused on gaining the love and acceptance of others. This false self may also develop narcissistic traits, such as a lack of empathy and a sense of entitlement, to protect the child from feeling the pain and vulnerability that the abuse and trauma have caused.

This may lead to a situation where the child's inner child and shadow self are in conflict, with the inner child seeking validation and attention while the shadow self feels unworthy and trying to hide.

Research has also shown that NPD may have a genetic component. Studies have found that certain genes may increase the likelihood of developing NPD, although the specific genes involved haven't been identified. Some researchers suggest that brain chemistry and structural differences play a role.

Moreover, societal and cultural factors also play a role in the development of narcissism. A culture that emphasizes individualism and self-promotion may lead to the development of narcissistic traits in some individuals. Additionally, some researchers suggest that societal changes, such as the rise of social media and the internet, where people are increasingly able to present a curated version of themselves to the world, may contribute to the development of narcissistic behavior.

Like any mental health condition, the causes of narcissism are complex and multi-faceted and can vary from person to person. Not everyone who exhibits narcissistic traits will meet the criteria for NPD diagnosis.

Recognizing Narcissistic Behavior in Yourself

Recognizing narcissistic behavior in yourself can be challenging, as it often involves confronting uncomfortable truths about yourself. However, it's an important step toward change.

Below are some warnings signs that you may be dealing with narcissistic behavior:

- An excessive need for attention and validation: You may find yourself constantly seeking validation from others, feeling hurt or angered when you don't receive it, and constantly needing to be the center of attention.

- A lack of empathy: You may have difficulty understanding or caring about the emotions of others and may be more focused on your own needs and wants.

- A need to control others: You may have a strong desire to control others through manipulation or force of will.

- Difficulty maintaining healthy relationships: You may have trouble maintaining long-term relationships or a pattern of exploiting others for your gain.

- A grandiose sense of self: You may have an inflated sense of your importance, talents, or abilities and may view yourself as superior to others.

- A tendency to blame others: You may blame others for your problems rather than take responsibility for your actions.

Remember that everyone has some narcissistic traits, it's only when these traits start to interfere with one's daily life and relationships that it becomes a problem, and only a professional can give a proper diagnosis.

It's also important to seek feedback from others. Ask friends and family members for their honest observations of your behavior, and be open to hearing their feedback, even if it's uncomfortable.

Remember that change is possible, but it takes hard work and commitment, and it's always better to seek professional help if you suspect you may have NPD.

Practical Steps for Change

Some narcissistic tendencies can indeed lead to an unhealthy lifestyle and outlook. However, it's also possible for narcissists to change their behavior to foster healthier relationships with others.

Narcissism doesn't have to be something that keeps someone from achieving peace and love within themselves or with those around them. By self-reflection and being open-minded about the possibility of making necessary changes, one can begin to embrace more positive behaviors and practices, such as letting go of toxic traits like envy and aggression. This could help a narcissist create meaningful connections instead of simply using people for personal gain or attention.

Ultimately, even though changing your mindset may take time and effort, it's much less damaging than allowing negative attitudes to persist indefinitely - resulting in lost opportunities for yourself and any potential partners you might meet along your journey.

Healing the inner child and doing shadow work can benefit a narcissist because it allows them to address and heal the underlying emotional wounds and traumas that led to the development of their narcissistic traits. By working through their past experiences and emotions, narcissists can learn to understand and accept their true selves rather than relying on the false self they've created to protect themselves.

Inner child work can involve identifying and connecting with the emotional needs and experiences of the inner child and learning to meet those needs healthily and appropriately. This can help the narcissist develop a more authentic sense of self and a greater capacity for empathy and vulnerability.

Shadow work explores and accepts the darker aspects of oneself, such as repressed emotions, thoughts, and feelings. By doing shadow work, a narcissist can learn to understand and integrate their shadow self, which can help ease feelings of shame and insecurity. It also allows them to take responsibility for their actions, learn to empathize with others, and develop more genuine relationships.

Changing narcissistic behavior is a difficult but possible task. It requires a willingness to confront uncomfortable truths about oneself and a commitment to making positive changes. While it may be difficult to change ingrained patterns of behavior, it's possible to progress with the right approach.

The steps outlined below are how you should start, but remember that change is a process that takes time.

1. Stop being the center of attention: Practicing humility and focusing on others' needs and perspectives can help reduce the need for constant validation and attention.

2. Let go of control: Learning to trust others and allowing them to make their own decisions can help reduce feelings of insecurity and the need to control every situation.

3. Build empathy skills: Practicing active listening, putting oneself in others' shoes, and developing a deeper understanding of their perspectives and emotions can help increase empathy.

4. Stop compulsive lying: Being honest and transparent in all interactions, reflecting on the reasons behind the lies, and learning to manage insecurities can help overcome compulsive lying.

5. Emotional dysregulation management: Identifying triggers, learning relaxation techniques, and practicing mindfulness can help manage intense or overwhelming emotions.

Game Plan

The following actions will empower you to break the cycle of self-centeredness in your relationships:

1. Recognize provocative situations:

   To stop acting like a narcissist, you must first identify what motivates you to do so. Perhaps you become irritated when you must wait in line for longer than you believe is reasonable or when someone tells you about their accomplishments and makes you feel inferior to them. The first step in changing your behavior is determining what causes you to behave this way.

2. Don't act immediately:

   You probably experience angry outbursts all the time if you always act in a way that matches your NPD. When you understand what causes you to be narcissistic, you may stop being that way by pausing when it occurs. Take a moment to count to 10 before you start yelling, insulting someone, or acting violently.

3. Consider how you would act in the best-case scenario:

   Consider how you would act in a perfect world if you were not self-centered. It's an excellent place to begin learning how to stop being a narcissist to think about how you'd like to act in different settings and with different people.

4. Consider the true reason for your self-centered behavior:

   What goes through your mind when you become angry? Do you have a negative self-image? Sad? Disappointed?

5. If you're angry, irritated, or disappointed, try changing your reaction:

Instead of concentrating your frustrations or stress on others, try to find other ways to cope. When you're anxious, you should take a minute to yourself, stop arguing with others, or do something to help you deal with your stress, such as exercise or meditation. Instead of becoming enraged as the argument becomes heated, consider telling the other person what's troubling you.

6. Consider how other people feel:

Narcissism stems from an inability to understand how other people feel. You may be accustomed to only caring about your feelings or point of view when in dispute or conflict. Instead of focusing only on yourself, attempt to see things through the eyes of others. You can't make someone feel better if you've injured them or made them sad. Consider how you'd feel in their shoes, and you might be able to grasp how they feel.

7. Begin apologizing:

You may not want to consider it, but if you have NPD, you have probably wounded many people in your life, possibly in the most horrible way. It's time to admit your mistakes and apologize for how you've been acting.

8. Identify your baggage:

Another fact about narcissists is that their behavior is often the result of unresolved pain. People with NPD can't cope with their grief and trauma. They instead pass it on to others. To overcome narcissism, you must recognize that you bring difficulties with you and that others are not always to blame.

9. Don't belittle others:

Because someone with NPD believes they're better than others, they'll put others down to make themselves feel better. Take the time to observe when you're doing this, and make a conscious effort to stop. Even if you believe you're superior to others, putting them down to make yourself feel better is a clue that you're not.

10. Assume everyone has good intentions:

Narcissists frequently believe that others are plotting against them or are simply being cruel to them because of how they feel. Instead of believing that others are out to get you, consider that they're regular individuals who encounter issues and disappointments the same way you do. They don't want you to be injured. Considering someone's good intentions will reduce your chances of becoming irritated with them.

11. Don't behave as you normally would:

Contrary to popular belief, doing the opposite of what you normally do can assist you in learning new habits rather than reverting to selfish ones. For example, if you tend to brag about what you've done, let others talk about what they've done without getting irritated or trying to "one-up" them. Feeling at peace with this is a significant step.

12. Be gentler with yourself:

This is crucial if you want to stop being a concealed narcissist. Covert narcissism is typically less visible, and research indicates that it's associated with self-attacks. Instead of being harsh on yourself for minor errors, try to be gentle with yourself.

13. Be considerate of others:

If you want to learn to be less self-centered, now is the time to do good things. Narcissism frequently leads to people acting in ways that exploit others. This means you're probably used to enticing others or making false promises to get them to do things for you. Stop doing this and instead do something nice for someone or something else without expecting anything in exchange. This could include shoveling a neighbor's driveway, washing your partner's laundry, or assisting a coworker at the office with a task.

14. Don't act on your emotions. Accept them instead:

Narcissistic people have difficulty dealing with unpleasant emotions such as anxiety, worry, and hurt feelings. When someone makes you feel awful, you should not insult, lash out, or try to retaliate in any manner. Instead, it would be best if you recognized that it's normal to feel lousy from time to time. Reacting negatively would only worsen matters.

15. Improve your listening skills:

    During a conversation, narcissists frequently return the spotlight to themselves. When someone else discusses a joyful recollection, an exciting event, or a significant accomplishment, you may feel compelled to discuss something greater or more interesting than what they did. To overcome narcissism, you must resist the impulse and exhibit interest in others. Instead of attempting to refocus their attention on you, ask them questions about what they're saying and listen to their responses.

16. Learn more about what you may be attempting to avoid:

    If you wish to treat your NPD, you should first identify the cause of the problem, no matter how unpleasant it may be. Consider the pain or trauma you're attempting to avoid. Is it anything you haven't discussed with your parents? What was the most painful rejection you ever experienced as a child? Whatever the case, getting to the bottom of it might help you understand why you behave the way you do.

17. Practice mindfulness:

    An individual with NPD may not realize that they have a pattern of conduct in which they instinctively feel they deserve special treatment and that others purposefully fail to provide them with the attention and praise they need. Break free from this habit of thinking and concentrate on the person you're with. Are they being impolite at the time, or do your regular patterns of thinking prevent you from seeing them? Mindfulness and meditation can help you and your partner communicate more effectively.

18. Accept that you must alter your beliefs:

    To stop being narcissistic, you must admit that you have lived your life from a distorted perspective that most people don't share. Once you understand this, you may begin to alter your thinking.

19. Give yourself time:

    Narcissism is a pattern of conduct that implies that it's ingrained in you. This means you can't expect to become less of a narcissist overnight. It will happen over time as you repeat the process.

20. Consult a therapist:

    Most of the time, it's difficult for somebody with NPD to improve independently. A therapist who understands how to address narcissism can help you establish whether you have distorted or unhelpful thought patterns that lead to undesirable behavior. A therapist can also help you set goals and deal with any trauma or unresolved problems that may make you act in a self-centered way. Behavior therapy becomes an important space to learn coping tools. A narcissistic personality disorder can also cause a variety of other issues, such as relationship problems, workplace issues, and a slew of other interpersonal issues. And therapy can be a place to learn how to manage these situations more healthily and reciprocally. It may also help you with other life challenges, including parenting, and it becomes an important space to build up that muscle of empathy that you've not been practicing in other areas of your life.

Maintaining Progress and Self-Improvement

Maintaining progress and self-improvement is an ongoing process that requires continuous commitment and effort. It requires a constant awareness of one's behavior and the ability to make adjustments as needed. Here are some practical steps that can help in maintaining progress:

1. Continual self-reflection and self-awareness:

   This is a process of regularly examining one's thoughts and actions and being open to learning from them. This can involve journaling, meditating, or working with a therapist to gain insight into one's behavior. It's important, to be honest with yourself, acknowledge when you have made a mistake, and take the time to understand why you made that mistake.

2. Staying accountable to others:

It's essential to have a support system, such as close friends and family members, or a therapist, who can provide guidance and support. Regularly sharing progress and discussing any difficulties can help make progress. Additionally, having people who can hold you accountable for your actions can help maintain progress.

3. Focusing on the well-being of others:

It's necessary to remember that narcissism is often characterized by a lack of empathy and a focus on one's own needs. One of the ways to counteract this is by actively focusing on the well-being of others. This can involve volunteering, reaching out to friends and family, or simply listening to others. Focusing on the well-being of others can help in developing empathy and compassion.

Remember that these steps are not a one-time thing but an ongoing process. Change takes time and effort, and it's important to be patient with yourself and not get discouraged if progress is slow.

Several habits and factors can hinder a narcissist's change or slow progress. Some of these include:

- Lack of insight: Narcissists often lack insight into their behavior and may resist recognizing that they have a problem. That's why they don't see the need for change and impede therapy progress.

- Resistance to feedback: Narcissists often have difficulty accepting feedback, particularly when it's critical. They may feel attacked or misunderstood, leading to defensiveness and a reluctance to change.

- Difficulty accepting responsibility: Narcissists blame others for their problems and may have difficulty accepting responsibility for their actions. This can make it hard for them to take steps toward change, as they may not see the need to do so.

- Lack of motivation: Narcissists may not see the value in changing their behavior, as they believe that their current way of thinking and acting is superior to others. This can make them less motivated to change.

- Difficulty in forming healthy relationships: Narcissists often have difficulty maintaining healthy relationships, making it harder for them to receive support and guidance in their progress. This can also make them feel isolated and unsupported, further hindering progress.

- Difficulty in accepting criticism: Narcissists may have difficulty accepting criticism, as they may view it as a threat to their self-esteem. They may react defensively or refuse to accept feedback, which can impede progress in therapy.

- Inability to empathize: Narcissists often have difficulty understanding or caring about the feelings of others, which can make it challenging for them to form healthy relationships. This lack of empathy can also make it difficult for them to understand the impact of their behavior on others, which can impede progress in therapy.

Defense mechanisms are psychological strategies that people use to protect themselves from feelings of anxiety, insecurity, and vulnerability. Narcissists, who often have fragile self-esteem, may use defense mechanisms to avoid facing their underlying insecurities and vulnerabilities.

Denial, for instance, is a defense mechanism where narcissists may deny or minimize the negative consequences of their behavior or blame others for their problems. Projection is another defense mechanism where narcissists may project their negative qualities onto others, accusing them of being selfish, dishonest, or controlling. Fantasy is a defense mechanism where narcissists may escape into a fantasy world where they're powerful, successful, and admired. Intimidation is a mechanism where narcissists may use threats or aggression to control others and avoid being challenged. Lastly, rationalization is a defense mechanism where narcissists may justify their behavior by making excuses or providing logical explanations for their actions.

These defense mechanisms can make it difficult for narcissists to change because they can't see their faults and take responsibility for their actions. They also can make them not open to criticism and feedback, which is often necessary for personal growth.

Additionally, when others point out their negative behavior, the narcissist can react with defensiveness, anger, and even hostility, which makes it difficult for them to form a healthy and meaningful relationship.

Spiritual Help in Healing?

Spirituality, which can include practices such as meditation, prayer, and self-reflection, can be beneficial in helping a narcissist to change. However, it's important to note that spirituality alone is unlikely to be sufficient in addressing the complex issues associated with NPD. It should be used in parallel with therapy and other forms of professional help. Additionally, not all people with NPD will have an interest or belief in spirituality, and different people may have different spiritual or religious beliefs. Therefore, it's important to understand that spirituality may not be suitable for everyone and should be tailored to their preferences and beliefs.

Spirituality can help a narcissist in several ways:

- Self-reflection: Spirituality often involves self-reflection, which can help a narcissist gain insight into their behavior and understand the underlying causes of their narcissism.

- Empathy and compassion: Spirituality can develop empathy and compassion, which can be beneficial in helping a narcissist understand the feelings of others and improve their relationships.

- Humility: Many spiritual practices emphasize humility, which can be beneficial in countering narcissists' tendency to view themselves as superior to others.

- Mindfulness: Spirituality can help develop mindfulness, which can assist a narcissist in being fully present and living in the moment, rather than constantly focusing on themselves.

We have reached the end of the book. I hope you have benefited from it and learned everything you need to get out of that web of narcissism. I wish you all the best and hope one day, your journal entry will say something like this:

"My narcissistic behavior had caused so much pain and hurt to those around me. I had always been so focused on getting what I wanted without considering the needs and feelings of others. But something inside of me had shifted ...

I realized that true happiness and fulfillment came from genuine connections with others, not just getting my way. I knew that to change, I needed to seek help. I found a therapist who specializes in working with individuals with narcissistic tendencies. Throughout our sessions, I learned about healthy communication and empathizing with others. I educated myself on the impact of narcissistic behavior and the importance of treating others with kindness and respect.

It wasn't easy, but with hard work and self-reflection, I started to see changes in myself. I apologized to those I had hurt and worked to rebuild relationships with friends and loved ones. As I looked around at the smiling faces of those gathered around me, I felt a sense of joy and peace that I had never experienced before. I finally learned that true happiness comes from treating others with love and respect.

I now know that change is possible and I'm determined to continue on this journey of self-improvement and to be the best version of myself."

Conclusion

In conclusion, being a narcissist can be detrimental to one's personal and professional relationships, and can lead to a lifetime of unhappiness and disappointment. However, with self-awareness, commitment, and hard work, it is possible to overcome narcissistic tendencies and develop a healthier and more fulfilling life.

The process of change starts with recognizing and admitting to the problem, then seeking professional help from a therapist or counselor who specializes in narcissistic personality disorder. Engaging in self-reflection, practicing empathy and active listening, and learning to accept criticism and feedback are also important steps in the journey of personal growth and transformation.

It is important to understand that change does not happen overnight, and that progress is often slow and gradual. However, with persistence and patience, anyone can learn to overcome their narcissistic tendencies and develop a more humble, compassionate, and fulfilling life.

Remember, you are not your behavior, and it is never too late to make a positive change in your life. Embrace the journey, be kind to yourself, and always keep moving forward towards a brighter, more fulfilling future.

Author's Note

Dear reader,

I hope you enjoyed my book.

Please don't forget to toss up a quick review on amazon, I will personally read it! Positive or negative, I'm grateful for all feedback. Reviews are so helpful for self-published authors and your feedback can make such a difference for my book!

Thanks very much for your time, and I look forward to hearing from you soon.

Sincerely,

Erik